Praise for
The Little Book of He and She

Wade Stevenson has created a book written by the body's desires, the mind's fascination with language, and the soul's deep longings. His work is poetic, profoundly beautiful, and eternally spiritual.

The story begins in mystery and ends with a moment of fascinating sensuality. I am beyond impressed and want to read everything this author has written and will write. His words are magical and will take your relationship to a new depth if you read the book together.

—Rebecca Johnson, The Rebecca Review

Buffalo-based author Wade Stevenson's slender volume of erotic fiction has no real beginning or end; it's more like a short ride on what he calls "the wheels of desire" with a nameless pair of eternal lovers. The language in this freewheeling, soul-bearing prose-poem sometimes recalls the trancelike repetition of Gertrude Stein and sometimes the work of more experimental writers, but it has a confident voice all its own.

—Ron Ehmke, *Buffalo Spree* magazine

Great little book, erotic and spiritual at the same time, it's really about a man's search for the Infinite, and in this way is a kind of modern-day "Song of Songs." A passionate biblical song about love and desire and the search for ultimate unity.

—Taylor Manning, Book Guru

ONE TIME IN PARIS

Other Books by Wade Stevenson

Ice Cream Parlors in Asia
Beds
The Colors of Love
The Little Book of He and She

ONE TIME IN PARIS

A Memoir of the 1960s

Wade Stevenson

Author of *The Little Book of He and She*

To Marty and Cheryl —

With Love —

Wade

iUniverse, Inc.

New York Bloomington Shanghai

ONE TIME IN PARIS
A Memoir of the 1960s

iUniverse books may be ordered through booksellers or by contacting:

iUniverse
1663 Liberty Drive
Bloomington, IN 47403
www.iuniverse.com
1-800-Authors (1-800-288-4677)

Because of the dynamic nature of the Internet, any Web addresses or links contained in this book may have changed since publication and may no longer be valid.

ISBN: 978-0-595-48658-8 (pbk)
ISBN: 978-0-595-48810-0 (cloth)
ISBN: 978-0-595-60754-9 (ebk)

Printed in the United States of America

Dedicated to: Lori, as always, and to

Annawade, Vanessa, Elie, Max and Ezra
in the hope that they may have the chance
to know the passion that inspired this book

Love gives naught but itself and takes naught but from itself. Love possesses not nor would it be possessed; For Love is sufficient unto love.

—Kahil Gibran

There is never any ending to Paris, and the memory of each person who has lived in it differs from that of any other.

—Ernest Hemingway

Contents

Author's Note xv

Chapter 1 1

Chapter 2 4

Chapter 3 7

Chapter 4 11

Chapter 5 13

Chapter 6 16

Chapter 7 20

Chapter 8 23

Chapter 9 28

Chapter 10 30

Chapter 11 34

Chapter 12 42

Chapter 13 45

Chapter 14 49

Chapter 15 51

Chapter 16 56

Chapter 17 63

Chapter 18 66

Chapter 19 68

Chapter 20 75

Chapter 21 78

Chapter 22 80

Chapter 23 84

Chapter 24 90

Chapter 25 94

Chapter 26 97

Chapter 27 103

Chapter 28 105

Chapter 29 107

Chapter 30 110

Chapter 31 113

Chapter 32 117

Chapter 33 120

Chapter 34 123

Chapter 35 127

Chapter 36 129

Chapter 37 132

Chapter 38 136

Chapter 39 138

Chapter 40 142

Chapter 41 146

Chapter 42 149

Chapter 43 151

Chapter 44 156

Chapter 45 160

Chapter 46 162

Chapter 47 164

Chapter 48 167

Chapter 49 170

Chapter 50 173

Chapter 51 175

Chapter 52 178

Author's Note

This memoir is based on certain experiences I lived in the 1960s. Names have been changed, characters combined, and events compressed. What I have tried to do, above all, is to convey the "truth of the heart."

CHAPTER 1

$\blacktriangledown$

The autumn I was nineteen I left for Paris. I went to find something new. My mother died before she forgave me for that. My father never spoke to me again.

It was in 1964. It was the year after Kennedy was assassinated.

For most of his life my father had been running a cutting machine factory in Buffalo, New York. He had inherited it from his own father. For years it had made no money, but, after WWII, it had started to work. Anyway, he felt successful, and that made him proud and stubborn. He had become convinced that his way was the right way, and that anyone else's way was a losing way. I didn't want to stick around, so, as soon as I could, I dropped out of college and got a job on an oil tanker that took me to Saudi Arabia and back and eventually to Paris via Le Havre.

In a dramatic all-night session before I left, my father let me know I was a loser. Even though I was the firstborn, he told me, it would be better if I had never been born. He told me I was like the first fish one catches—he never should have accepted me, but thrown me back in the water.

Of course I hated him passionately for that, as well as for a few other things. I vowed never to return. And didn't.

Before we get into my Paris story, I should tell you that, for most of my adolescent life, I had been falling in and out of love with women. It would be too easy to explain that tendency by telling you that polio had paralyzed my mother's legs, and an accident (she had fallen down the stairs) had made her arms almost useless. There was never a question of the slightest contact of any physical kind with her. I was raised by a succession of nannies. My mother remained distant, unobtainable—at best a symbol, at worst a phantom. You could say that this maternal absence was the cause of my early troubles, and it might be partly true. Yet I had always felt something else that I thought went deeper than that, was rooted in a more profound source. It was more like a soulful yearning, a longing to find the one woman who would correspond to me in a true way, and who could help me become the man I was destined to be. Perhaps it was no more than a simple desire for happiness, but I was convinced that, if I had any chance of finding it, it would be in the arms and body of a woman.

Of course, I had no knowledge of Cynthia then, or of what the reality of being in love with her would ultimately cost me.

My first "love" was a girl I met in a horse barn. I was working there in the summer and had had a "crush" on her for some time. She was braiding the tail of a big, black jumper. I entered the stall. It smelled of hay and manure. I stood behind her. I was not yet sixteen. I felt something big and strong rise in me. It was stronger than any feeling I had ever known before. It was there, it was real, it pressed me out relentlessly from my old self toward the new self that was in a space of a few inches between myself and her tight blue-jeaned buttocks as she braided the tail of the big, beautiful, black jumper. What was happening? When would it happen? Where would it lead me?

It surprised me that she did not move when I touched her. Was she expecting it? Perhaps. She let me slip off her shirt. Then her breasts were bare and I gingerly touched the tips. They stiffened. Her back arched. Her fingers continued their work of deftly braiding the sleek hair strands, holding clumps of tail and weaving the ends together. She did not look back, she did not move, she said nothing. She braided.

I was wearing jeans. I lowered them and rubbed against her. It ended suddenly. The memory of it lingered for a long time.

Years later I can look back and say: My real life began in a barn stall.

What do I remember about Buffalo? I was always restless. My first memory is thinking, *I've got to get out of here!*

Get out of what?

Get out of a crib, out of a playroom, out of a kindergarten—and later, out of a structure, a family, a psychiatric ward, a university, a place.

When I was six years old I escaped from first grade, and my father had to send the police to find me and bring me back.

At the age of eight I started to make maps and drawings of imaginary countries I wanted to travel to—strange islands, often populated by wild women.

There was a shipwreck; everyone perished. I had to swim hundreds of yards ashore. On the beach there was a lithe-limbed woman with dark hair urging me toward the safety of sand, the warm knowledge of her thighs. She did not live alone; hundreds of other women inhabited that island. I became their friend, their mascot, their willing captive. They fed me, gave me milk, and I nourished them with the honey of my young manhood.

At the age of ten I made a desperate attempt to escape from my family's summer house in Southampton, Long Island, and ride my bicycle to New York City. The cops caught up with me somewhere near Hampton Bays and brought me back, shame-faced and fuming at my failure. I was punished and told I would soon be dispatched to boarding school. I didn't care. All I wanted was to disappear, to flee, to escape, to find an "elsewhere" I could finally call my own. I was in a headlong rush to become the victim of my future.

CHAPTER 2

▼

Days and years went by.

I lived in restless hope, with a constant feeling of reckless, sullen, insatiable rebellion.

My father had made another bad choice and concluded that his life would be significantly easier if I were sent to boarding school. So one September day, at the ripe age of thirteen, I was driven to and dropped off at St. Paul's School in Concord, New Hampshire. It was a very conservative school at that time. I more than hated it, and did everything I could to escape or to be expelled. I almost succeeded, but that would be another story.

In the summertime I sold newspapers and washed dishes. I worked around horses, digging out muck from stalls. One night in a shed at the racetrack, some dark-colored groom held me down with a knife pressed next to my throat and tried to rape me. My anger and rage grew. I had to find something but I didn't know what or where. And don't forget: I didn't know anything. I was a stupid young kid. I had no one to help me and no one to turn to.

I never held a job for more than a few months.

My father cursed me and repeated that I was a "no-good loser."

My mother Mary Louise was from an upper-class New York society family. When she was eighteen she contracted polio and nearly died from it. She underwent "the iron lung" and spent years recovering in Warm Springs, Georgia, where she became friendly with Franklin Roosevelt. I still have some photos of them sitting next to each other in wheelchairs. She had visited Paris once as a little girl, and she would talk wistfully about those days. It was her dream to see Paris again, but she couldn't travel because of the condition of her legs. And later there was the accident that crippled her arms. She regretted Paris, where she had lived for a short time as a child. She talked seriously about moving back there, when I knew there was never any real hope of her actually doing so. My father dominated her life completely. She was crippled. She couldn't even go to the bathroom unless he helped her.

Here's the problem: I never knew why I was alive.

One day I told my mother, "You know, it would be much better for me if I had never been born."

She burst into tears.

Still, when my father came home, she told him what I had said and he dragged me into the laundry room and walloped me with his belt. It hurt. I never forgave him.

Angrily, I plotted day and night of how I would escape. I thought, *When the spring comes again, I will get on a boat and go to Paris.*

Summer came. I lay on my back in a field of grass after midnight and watched the night sky. I knew I was alone and liked it. I inhaled the vast darkness. There were no clouds, and the stars shone as if they had just been minted in silver.

It was 1961.

The hit song that summer was by the crooner Johnny Mathis, "Chances Are."

I smoked Lucky Strikes and made some money off the guys at the barn by pitching coins and placing two-dollar bets on long-shot horses at the Fort Erie Race Track.

I planned to go to Paris as soon as I had enough money to get to New York City and buy third-class passage on a transatlantic steamer. I imagined myself arriving in Le Havre, totally penniless but full of hope.

My intense desire for women, or for "A Woman," never went away, and I masturbated two or three times a day to endless fantasies of what it would finally be like.

I came very close with Cissy, a twenty-four-year-old girl from South Carolina. She had been exercising her horse at the stable and I noticed her long legs and southern charms. Later we went to a bar and were drinking Singapore slings, and she said, "You know that big drive-in movie we saw on the highway coming here? Let's go there."

She had a white Chevrolet with tail fins, and we hung the speakers on the rolled-down windows and sat in the backseat. I moved toward her, pushing very close, but she said she wanted to watch the movie, and please just leave her alone.

But, putting her body "at play," she stretched out full-length on the backseat, asking me to move, so she could put her legs up. I was kneeling on the floor, and I touched her hand and was thrilled.

Somehow, a used tennis ball appeared. She raised her legs, and I started rolling the tennis ball from her loins down the sweet slope of her bare legs, slowly on her cool thighs, past her knees, down to her ankles. Then I reversed the motion, and rolled the ball tenderly back up again, pushing it very slowly, trying to make it go as slowly as I could, urging the fuzzy tennis ball to be patient with me, to accept my game, and to have her accept my game. And she did.

I could tell she liked it, was participating, as she arched her back, accentuating the angle of her legs, lifting up her knees, forcing me to press the yellow ball harder into that sweet spot area at the apex of her lovely, lonely thighs, which closed and joined together at the very last moment, protecting their dark and beautiful mystery.

Just when my excitement was peaking and radical and revolutionary thoughts had taken control of my whole being, she suddenly clasped my wrist, stopping the pressing-in movement I was seeking to exert, my fingers splayed wide, as I was trying to wedge her thighs even a few inches apart. She said, "I'd like some popcorn, honey, will you be an angel and go get it for your sweet Cissy?"

She laughed. Her laughter clung to her lips, not wanting to leave her husky throat.

I got the popcorn. Yellow-white kernels spilled out of the bucket, falling over the edge of the backseat, littering the floor. I picked out the best pieces and delicately and languorously inserted them between her half-opened lips.

That was all. Nothing else happened. It was a night of popcorn and foamy cheap beer and endlessly rolling the tennis ball up and down the long, smooth canyon my hands had helped create between her thighs.

CHAPTER 3

▼

I had briefly attended college at the University of California at Berkeley. I had wanted to go to California because California was different and it was as far away from Buffalo and my father as I could reasonably get at that time.

I was still fighting and lusting on the edge of a rebellion I wasn't yet able to control.

I ended up in a rooming house run by a crippled man in a wheelchair and his deaf wife of over forty years. He would wheel himself around the dim hallways, mumbling, "You know, kid, I always say, you know, what's good for the goose is good for the gander. Remember that, kid!"

I shared a room with a lanky red-haired freshman who had puncture marks all over his arms. He told me he wanted to keep the room dark, the shades constantly drawn, and he spent most of the day sprawled half-naked across the bed. When evening came he arose and went into action, roaming the streets in search of a "hit."

I loaned him money, and, when that ran out, he had me go with him to the local Red Cross building a few times a week and sell our blood for $5 or $10 in cash, which he immediately spent.

It was blood for drugs, and I learned to hate it and never wanted anything more to do with it. I knew I had to get out of that situation, and then something happened that prompted my escape.

I had fallen in love with my German teacher. Her name was Ute, and she came from northern Germany. She was a strong, muscular woman with short, dark hair.

She reminded me of a Teutonic warrior with beautiful breasts and shapely hips designed to lure naïve souls to their doom.

After class she would invite me to her house in the Berkeley hills and she would read me poetry by Herman Hesse and Rainer Maria Rilke. I was from Buffalo; I was a country boy. It was the first time I had heard poetry like that. It stirred me deeply. Even today I can remember her soft, husky voice as she sat on the sofa with me, held my hand, and read Hesse's haunting poem:

"How strange it is
Alone in the mists to wander!
To live is to be solitary.
No man knows another,
Each is alone."

Or Rilke's prophetic words:

"He who has not loved now, will never love.
He who now has no home, will never have a home."

I listened to her voice and intently watched the pear-shaped forms that I imagined were struggling for freedom beneath her cotton shirt.

One afternoon she said to me, "Do you know how to say 'I love you' in German?"

"Yes," I said.

"*Ich liebe dich*," she said. "But I don't like the way it sounds in German. In French it's much nicer. Do you know it in French?"

"I never took French," I said.

"*Je t'aime*," she said. "Say it."

But I couldn't say it. I didn't want to say it to her. I wanted to tell her I couldn't continue with her. It had to stop. She wouldn't let me do anything but sleep with her. It may seem odd, but that was driving me crazy.

Three times a week I had to sit in class and patiently listen to her teach the rudiments of German grammar.

Afterwards she would invite me back to her house in the Berkeley hills and we would sit on the couch and she would take my hand and put it under her blue cotton shirt and urge me to say *"Ich Liebe Dich Sehr,"* and other, deeper, stranger-sounding words I didn't understand.

One day after class she said she needed to talk to me. She said she couldn't see me any more. She said, "You think you love me but you don't. You're just in love with an image of me. That's why I can't be with you. It's begun to really annoy me! It's the third time it's happened in my life! The third time, imagine that! You're so young—it's just a matter of time before you won't want to see me any more. So I'm cutting it off now. Good-bye."

I remembered back to the day when I was a little boy and I had to move in with my grandmother because my mother could not take care of me due to the almost complete paralysis of her legs, and my father was too busy trying to keep his cutting machine factory out of bankruptcy.

I remembered that night and outside the sudden sound of the police cars and fire engines wailing by in the vast and dangerous night.

I remembered my grandmother saying, "Some day your mother will be better and she'll want to take you back and I'm going to have to give you up."

I was already looking for something that I knew in my heart would be impossible to find: the security of staying with one person in one place for an undetermined length of time.

I would pass Ute's house on those late fall mornings on the way to the university. I saw the front porch and the shutters and the old brown couch where we had sat in our first days of euphoria. But now there were cobwebs on the railing and a smell of dampness and mildew.

I walked into the crowded classroom and I moved conspicuously to the front row where I sat looking fixedly at Ute.

She was speaking slowly in German, explaining this word and that word, this text and that text. I paid no attention to what she was saying. I just watched her. My heart was pounding between my thighs. Would she look up and recognize me? Would she acknowledge me or not?

This had to be the moment of instant and spell-binding recognition. It had to be the moment when she looked up and saw me and knew that I was there for her.

But I knew immediately and without a doubt that this was not going to happen. She would never look up at me. She would never stop reading her German texts in that slow, lyrical, but ponderous manner she had. She would never acknowledge, recognize, or truly love me in the way that I wanted or sensed it should be.

A part of me said, "This is your life and it's happening, pay attention!"

Another part answered, "Bullshit! It's time to split!"

As I walked out of that classroom for the last time, I didn't look back. The shock waves multiplied in little beats beneath my chest.

A few days later I went to the bus terminal in San Francisco and took a Greyhound cross-country back to New York City. As I sat on the bus and watched the great American landscape whirl by, I stupidly thought: *You are at last alone. There is now no love, no chance of feeling. You are free to achieve the perfect clarity of nothingness.*

But it didn't happen that way.

CHAPTER 4

▼

Of course, leaving Berkeley in that way and coming back to New York City on the Greyhound bus did not exactly please my father. He told me if I didn't go back to college, he was going to cut me off completely, disinherit me—in short, I would have nothing. I had no idea what I was going to do. I knew I couldn't go back, but I had no idea how I was going to go forward either.

My father suggested I should go see a friend of his, a doctor in a hospital, who was skilled in dealing with troubled adolescents. He was going to give me some tests, I was told, so they could figure out what my aptitudes were, what I might be good at doing, what possibly the future might hold in store for me.

So one bright, promising early summer morning in June, I agreed, and he went with me. We took a taxi and arrived at one of those big imposing New York City hospitals.

"You're going to take some tests," he said. "It'll take a few hours. I'll come back and get you later."

And he left and I was alone on the fourth floor with the doctor and some nurses. Someone said, "We're going up to the fifteenth floor, that's where we do the tests. So, let's go."

We filed into the elevator and I wondered why two or three male nurses had entered with the doctor. As soon as the elevator doors closed, they seized my arms and put a kind of straitjacket on me, with me struggling and screaming. Suddenly, but too late, I realized what was going on. When we got out on the fifteenth floor, they dragged me by both arms to a barred room with a sight glass through the door so they could observe me. They strapped me onto a narrow bed and gave me some injection so that I passed out, cursing my father and family and vowing that never again would I make the mistake of trusting them or of asking for their help.

The hospital stay was quite an ordeal. The doctors put me on suicide watch; I was drugged and physically constrained. A psychiatric aide advised me that, if I had any hope of getting out of that institution quickly, it would be in my best interests to comply. In other words, since they thought I was crazy, I had to pretend to be "crazy," because, if I insisted that there was nothing wrong with me, they interpreted that as a sign and proof of my sickness. Even when I went to the bathroom, a nurse would accompany me, to make sure "nothing happened." With sadness and anxiety, I saw other patients, many of whom were truly sick, wandering up and down the long corridors like pale tormented ghosts.

One sultry August evening, while I was resting on my simple cot in my cell-like room, I heard a stream of notes that seemed to float by my barred windows. Someone on the floor above me, or farther down the corridor, was playing the flute. The notes were piped with a soft, plaintive intensity. In my altered state, I could feel the suffering the melody expressed and I could identify with it. I felt one with it. The playing went on for a long time in a wistful, penetrating way. The flute music stirred my spirit, and I took it as a secret sign that someone wanted to save me. I determined to do everything I could to get out of that place as quickly as possible.

The next day I asked one of the nurses who had been playing the flute. She frowned as if I had breached some rule, but finally said it was a "troubled girl" who had arrived a few days earlier. Her name was Cynthia.

After some months, the hospital doctors, in their infinite wisdom, decided there was nothing seriously wrong with me, and, although my father argued against it, I was released on the condition that I would go back to college. Instead, I got a job working as a mail clerk at the Cunard Steamship Lines in New York City. From there I managed to find work as a deck hand on an oil tanker with an all-Italian crew that took me via Ras Tanura in the Persian Gulf half-way around the world, and finally back to Le Havre, France, where I decided I'd had enough of the sea-faring life.

CHAPTER 5

▼

The Gare du Nord, late afternoon. I had arrived by train from Le Havre. I had a duffel bag with me and little else. I managed to find the taxi queue and waited in line and I wondered what I would do next. Actually, I had no idea. The driver opened the door and asked me in French where I wanted to go. I didn't know any French at that time, so I wasn't able to answer. I had thought that, since he was a taxicab driver and used to dealing with foreigners, he might know some English.

When we were approaching the Pont du Carrousel bridge near the Louvre museum, he again asked me where I wanted to go.

I said, "Take me someplace interesting."

"Comprends pas," he said. "Don't understand."

"Anywhere where there's something happening," I said. I knew there was a lot of "life" in Paris. I just had to find it.

The cab driver, a small swarthy type, suddenly stopped the car as we were passing by the Louvre. On the right side of me I could see the obelisk of the place de la Concorde framed by the Arc de Triomphe. On the other side, was that wonderful sculpture of a falling woman, precariously balanced, her arms raised as if in shock or protest, by the French artist, Aristide Maillol.

"Sortez, monsieur, sortez!" the cab driver was yelling at me. "Get out! Get out!"

Before I could move, he came around to the side of the cab, opened the door, grabbed me, pulled me out, and threw me and my brown duffel bag on the pavement. He drove away cursing me loudly before I had a chance to pay him or do anything.

Welcome to Paris.

I had always been good at writing, so I thought I might write a book. Many writers before me, such as Hemingway and Fitzgerald and Ezra Pound, had come to Paris to do that, and I felt their ghosts were everywhere. Maybe, I thought, in some way I could try to do the same. True, it was the 1960s and not the 1920s, and there was no more "lost generation," but it was also true that, if you were nineteen years old in 1964, one of the best places in the world to be had to be Paris. And I was there.

I moved into a seedy hotel near St. Sulpice. My room on the top floor had ceilings that echoed the shape of the building's mansard roof. There was a shared Turkish-style toilet off the corridor. I could open my window and see the slate blue rooftops of Paris. The room cost me fifty francs a day, which was about ten dollars at that time, and I had only a few hundred dollars in my pocket—but I didn't care. It made absolutely no difference to me. I was free and alone and in the world's most beautiful city at last. It was a city of many fine things—of sensuality and light and love and art, and all these aspects were there waiting to be discovered. They had been there a long time, and many people had discovered them before, but now it was my turn. It was between Paris and me, and I knew already that I would find a way to survive.

And I did survive—on baguettes and camembert and cheap wine. Like that character in Dostoyevsky's *The Idiot*, I lived in silence, I didn't speak to anyone. In fact, I couldn't speak to anyone because I didn't know any French. I didn't know how long I would stay in Paris. It might be another week—and it was always possible that another week would become ten years.

Paris is made up of twenty neighborhoods called *arrondissements*, and I thought the best way to get to know Paris would be to live for a time in each one. So I moved around like a gypsy from one to another, from the Bois de Boulogne to the Bois de Vincennes, and from the Right Bank to the Left Bank, never staying in one place for more than three or four nights.

I got a job working for the *Herald-Tribune* selling newspapers on the Champs-Elysées, just like that character the actress Jean Seberg played in Godard's great movie, *Au Bout de Souffle*. I would pick up the new day's edition of the *Herald-Tribune* at their offices on rue de Berri and I would hawk it down all the cafés on the Champs-Elysées. During the day I read French books and went to French movies and learned enough French so that I could talk well enough to the customers in the cafés so they would buy the paper from me.

Later, when the waiters came out with their brooms, and the tables and chairs were cleaned, carried inside, and stacked, I would return the unsold papers to the *Herald-Tribune* offices on rue de Berri; then I would run back down the

Champs-Elysées, all the way to the place de la Concorde, past the Egyptian obe-lisk, and then over the bridge and past the ghostly Senate Building and down the boulevard St Germain until I came to the boulevard Raspail, and running as fast as I could I would continue all the way to the boulevard Montparnasse, where sometimes I would stop at the The Coupole brasserie or The Dome restaurant and have a beer, a *demi*, and a late-night snack.

I had no contact at all with my mother or father, but my grandmother from New York City wrote me and said she was sending a few hundred dollars in a money order to me care of American Express, 11, rue Scribe.

CHAPTER 6

▼

And so it happened that one day I presented myself at the offices of the American Express, 11, rue Scribe. A clerk told me the mail services were on the third floor. It was very hot. I stood in line for a long time. Finally I was able to show my passport and receive the money order my kind grandmother had sent me from New York City. This was a life-saving event for me at the time, and I was thankful and grateful to her for that gesture. Feeling good about everything, once again in tune with life and all its possibilities, I got back in the elevator to go down to the ground floor. Just as the elevator door closed, a tall slender girl with blonde hair and laughing blue eyes entered. She looked at me in astonishment, her eyes surprise-shocked. We were squeezed together in the elevator along with lots of other back-packing Americans, but I could feel her surprise, as if she were saying, "Is that you? I can't believe we're meeting in this way!"

It was strange to meet here there, totally by chance, on the elevator between floors in the American Express building. Certainly I could not forget the girl I had glimpsed like a phantom in the corridors, the girl who had played such tender wistful melodies to me on her silver flute from the room down the hall when I was locked up in the psych ward of that hospital in New York City. I think we both knew at once when we met each other like that, brought together by fate, that it would not be easy for us to leave each other again, and that our separate histories were going to be bound together in some intimate and unfathomable way. And that is exactly what happened, and what the rest of this story is about.

From then on it became clear to me that I was not going to be able to leave Paris until I had lived the adventure of Cynthia. It wasn't enough for me to be alone any more. It wasn't enough simply to be taking the green autobuses and standing in the open area at the back and not caring if I was lost or where the autobus finally ended up. I had to find some way to move forward and renew myself. In the notebook I kept at the time, I wrote:

I cannot go on living like this. It's true the solitude troubles me, but it's not only the fact that I am alone. I feel that I need to find out something about love and relationships, and my future now depends on my being able to do that.

So many people now are talking revolution, about being on the cutting edge of music and art and life, about how the '60s will be a complete rupture with the past—maybe so, but I have to find my own way in all this. Destiny or karma has brought me together with the girl with the magic silver flute again, and I must see where that goes, follow that path to the end.

The next time I saw Cynthia it was at a private party given on a spacious rooftop balcony in Montmartre a stone's throw away from the Moulin Rouge. She had given me the address and told me to meet her there after midnight. I had known from the first glimpse we'd had of each other in that hot, cramped elevator at American Express that we were destined to see each other again.

This déjà-vu feeling of having known her before as in some past life would haunt me for a long time.

Of course, I had never been to Paris before, so it was strange to me how, from the moment of my arrival at the Gare du Nord that day, when the taxicab driver had thrown me and my duffel bag out on the street on the Pont Carrousel bridge, how instantly I had felt at home. One of the nice things about Paris was that everyone left you alone. You could go out to cafés and restaurants or walk the sidewalks at night and no one paid any attention to you or cared who you were or where you came from. In Paris you could live like a stranger, totally anonymous. You could live or die, you could fall in or out of love—no one cared, no one would ever know. And that suited me just fine.

Cynthia this time was dressed in black. Her blonde hair was swept back. She looked solemn, mysterious, distant. She had slender hips and a willowy shape. For a moment I was afraid she would not recognize me.

But she said, "Hey, you're the guy I met at American Express and who was locked up in that looney-bin with me. I felt so sad for you, because I heard how you'd been brought in there, trapped, against your will."

I nodded.

"I bet you're a Scorpio," she said.

"A Scorpio, yes. How did you know?"

"I know," she said, "because I felt from those days in the hospital that you have a wounded heart, a wounded Scorpio heart. I'm Aquarius," she went on. "Scorpio and Aquarius ... that could be interesting."

"You look beautiful tonight," I told her. "I've never seen you so dressed up."

"I like to wear black," she said. "You know why? I feel it helps me control my madness!"

I did not know or care then if she was mad. I didn't know what type of madness she suffered from or where it would lead me, or if one day it would hurt those who came into contact with her and became close to her.

But, since I had this strange feeling that I had known her "forever," I didn't waste any time and immediately asked Cynthia if she wanted to come back to my hotel room with me. It was getting late, the last show at the Moulin Rouge was over, and people were streaming out onto the dark shiny pavements below us.

Cynthia gave me a sense of urgency I could not explain. It was like a life-force, pushing me to do something with her, to go forward, regardless of consequences.

She looked at me without comment, simply said that she lived near the zoo, in the fifth arrondissement, that she shared an apartment with Pierre, a French fashion photographer who worked for *Elle* magazine.

"He's just a friend," she added. "Still, no doubt he's waiting for me. So I should stop there to tell him I'm going out."

In those days there were no cell phones or e-mails, and even landline phones were hard to come by. I wondered who Pierre was and what she had meant by "friend." We hailed a taxi near the place Pigalle without difficulty and drove down the long, globe-lighted avenues past the opera and the place de la Concorde and then over one of the many bridges that cross the Seine, until we got to a small side street near the Jardin des Plantes, a botanical garden that also housed a menagerie.

I waited in the cab while she rang the buzzer on one of those old French buildings that look like they're squeezed in a sandwich between other buildings, and then the lights went on in the staircase and she went upstairs. She had not pressed my hand or looked at me as she left the cab. I wasn't sure if she would come back down again. Perhaps Pierre would not so easily let her go. So far she had not shown any sign of a real or true feeling for me at all. From the other side of the street came the rank smell of the animals. I thought of Rilke's beautiful poem about the panthers pacing up and down in their cage. In my heart I felt something new—it was like a wild and restless ache. It made me long to reach out and do something hard and physical. What I did not want to do was to wait in the backseat of the cramped French taxi for Cynthia to decide whether she was going to come back down and go to my hotel room with me or not.

The taxi driver was getting upset too; he growled in a surly way that either I had to give some instructions as to where we were going and when, or I could get out of the cab and wait. Many people said the French were unfriendly, and it was true. I started to get out because I did not feel like getting into a bi-lingual shouting match with the taxicab driver. I had no fondness for French taxicab drivers, especially after being so unceremoniously dumped in the street on my arrival in Paris. A few moments later Cynthia reappeared with a smile and told me that everything was okay.

"Sorry, but Pierre wasn't there, I had to leave a note for him. He gets so upset if he doesn't know where I am. You can understand, can't you?"

I wondered, did she also tell him in her note whether she was going to come back later that night or not?

CHAPTER 7

▼

9, rue Campagne-Irè. At the end of the passageway, I had rented a small room. It was underneath the ground level so that when you opened the grilled window and looked up, you could see only the shoes and legs of the people walking by. Picasso was supposed to have lived once at this address. I was embarrassed to show it to Cynthia because it was so small—something like a room in a cellar. There was basically a bed, a tiny kitchen, a bathroom with no shower, and a tight living area.

I had a bottle of the new Beaujolais, which was cool and good, and I went to uncork it and asked Cynthia if she wanted some. But she said no, she was fine. She sat on the edge of my bed, her long, svelte legs coiled under her. She looked at me curiously, half-expectantly. I knew already that I was powerfully drawn to her, but I didn't want to make the mistake I had made with other girls—trying to get them to surrender too quickly. On the one hand, I had no real experience of love and wanted to find out what it was; on the other, I did not want to cheapen the idea I had of it by committing to it as if to some form of gymnastic exercise. It had to go further than that, be raised to another plane—a higher power of desire.

"I know you so little," I said. "There was just that one afternoon when I ran into you in the corridor of that psych hospital in New York City. And then, when you played your flute, I could sometimes hear the notes through the bars of my window."

"Yes," she said, "you're right. If we're going to get to know each other, maybe we should start by asking the most simple questions."

I brushed aside my impatience and my strong nascent feeling that meeting Cynthia was truly a case of "shock love." Instead I asked, "So where are you from?"

She was from a small paper mill town in northern New Hampshire, she answered. She had come to Paris on a music scholarship to study the flute with Jean-Pierre Rampal. But she had quickly realized that she would never be good enough to satisfy the personal level of her expectations. It would bitterly disappoint her parents, she said, but she could not continue playing the flute with the illusion that she was better than she was. So she had stopped.

She had then spent a few months traveling with Ode. "She came from a little desert town south of Agadir in Morocco, near the Saharan border, where the famous 'Blue Men'—the camel traders—live."

"How did you meet Ode?"

"She was an assistant on one of the fashion photo shoots I was doing. And we hit it off really well from the beginning, Ode and I."

Cynthia's mother was half French, so Cynthia spoke French fluently. She spoke the language so clearly and with such perfect enunciation, it was difficult to tell she was an American. I liked to listen to her smooth, crystalline voice. I knew I could learn from her, and I was hungry to learn.

"After a while it hit me that hitchhiking through Europe and North Africa with Ode was not my cup of tea," she said, laughing. She had a fresh, smooth, somewhat girlish laughter that reminded me of the long blonde color of her flowing hair.

Her fine hair streamed over her shoulders and, even though it stopped a few inches below her breast, it somehow seemed to be connected to the well-defined curve of her haunches and shapely legs. Cynthia was charming without being aware of her charm. I could not help wondering how long it would be before the knowledge of the fascination she aroused in me would become apparent to her as well.

Right now I was just happy to know her, in this precise moment of time. I felt a terrible sense of excitement for her as well as a yearning for her body.

This desire expressed itself in an intangible way that hurt me inexplicably.

I walked around Cynthia a few times, circling the bed, sipping the red wine, talking to her about the day's events in Paris. An unread copy of the *Herald-Tribune* lay on my desk next to a well-leafed paperback in French of André Breton's surrealistic novel *Najda*.

Cynthia watched me like a cat, amused and curious, maintaining her distance in semi-silence. Then she pranced into the bathroom and I heard her locking the door behind her. I sat down and browsed the *Herald-Tribune* but could not find anything of interest. There was an article about a hot British rock group, The Beatles, who were about to tour the United States. My mind was on Cynthia and on what might happen between us.

She re-emerged from the tiny bathroom and made a mocking formal bow.

She danced a few steps past me, letting her fingertips run over my hair just long enough so that I felt in my heart that renewed painful sensation of wanting her. I moved to kiss her but she spun away.

"I have to go now," she said abruptly.

"But you just came," I protested.

"Come and go, come and go, that's what I do. *C'est la vie.* That's life," she said. She smiled in a rueful, half-knowing way.

"But can't you stay just a little bit longer? Here, I'll make some coffee. We can sit and talk some more and you can tell me about your adventures in Morocco with Ode."

"No, no, no. I don't drink coffee, and my photographer friend will be most upset if I don't show up soon."

"So Cinderella has to get home before dawn?"

"No, but it's better like this, really," she assured me with a bright engaging glance that promised hope but left nothing behind it.

"When will I see you again?"

"Next Friday, if you like. I have to go to the Bois de Boulogne to do a photo shoot in the morning, but in the afternoon we can meet at a friend's place there. She has a nice studio, and we can have tea there and talk some more. I really feel we need to talk to each other ... there are so many things to say!"

I wondered what she meant by that and why she was inviting me to her friend's studio apartment near the Bois de Boulogne. Clearly, she must have some feeling for me, or else her invitation would not have gone so far. With my heart trembling with an anticipation I had not felt in a long time, I kissed her gently on both cheeks and let her go.

CHAPTER 8

▼

I did not see Cynthia again for a few weeks. My grandmother sent me another letter with a modest money order and wrote that I should not continue to waste my life in Paris, but I should return to New York without delay. She said, if I came back, my parents were ready to forgive me for my flight and escape. They would take me back as if nothing had happened and I could resume my studies at Harvard University, where, surprisingly, I had been accepted.

I didn't answer that letter. I had no phone. It was impossible to reach me except by mail. I even had my mailing address changed to *"poste restante"* (general delivery) at the nearest local post office. There were many things I still had to work out. Returning to the States was out of the question.

I spent a long time lying on the bed I had bought for a few francs at one of the many flea markets. I would smoke a Gitane cigarette and watch the cracks in the ceiling (I got to know every fissure intimately). I would open the heavy metal window grills and look up and watch the procession of smartly-dressed shoes passing by on the pavement above me. It was somehow fitting that my contact with the universe started with people's shoes, not their faces.

Sometimes I would go out and wander aimlessly down the long tree-lined boulevard Raspail. Cars shot by me in streaks and pinpoints of light. I wondered where Cynthia was and what she was doing. I sent her a few letters asking her to meet me at various rendezvous points, but she never answered.

I lived simply, careful not to spend any more money than absolutely required. I lived on peanuts and cheese and bread, and drank tap water and cheap red wine.

Solitude became heavy and weighed upon me, especially since I had met Cynthia. She had promised, with her excellent French and social skills, to introduce me to a whole new world of light and laughter and people. But so far that had not happened, and I felt a deep pain inside myself, an aching void, a real misery.

It seemed to me that everything I had done—or hadn't done—so far in my life no longer meant anything to me. What I wanted was hard to describe, but I knew it was of a rarer nature and order, incomparably different. Even when my own angst-ridden tapes spun around in my mind, I found them to be boringly artificial. My thoughts just kept wandering over to Cynthia, to her svelte, curved, ethereal body.

She had appeared out of nowhere in my life like an apparition, a vision, a dream. I knew that I had to have her, but my desire to possess her was rooted in the physical. At the same time, however, whatever it was that powered me toward her transcended the physical in a new and surprising way.

One day, as if by magic, Cynthia called and suggested I meet her at a photography studio in Neuilly.

One of my teachers in high school had written my family a note about me, saying, "He's very high-strung, self-willed, impetuous, and vulnerable."

The shrink they had sent me to see commented, "He's like a burned-out volcano, seething with the lava of all these pent-up emotions, which could break out and erupt at any time."

The one friend I had made at St. Paul's School, who was later killed in the Vietnam War, had even called me in Paris to warn me, "What you need, man, is some center, something you can relate to, before you go fucking crazy. You're just being pulled in too many different directions."

I knew they all were right: I needed a stable centering point, a clear filter that would help me strain and sort out the fragmented memories and terrible violent threads that ran through my life.

Now, in Paris, caught up with the Cynthia obsession, the thought came to me that I was losing my ability to control what was happening.

On the other hand, with the help of Cynthia and her many friends (like Ode, whom I hadn't yet met), I felt I might be able to extend the limits of my own mind into new and different realms. That was the one legitimate hope left to me. I had to try to do it, and to do it purely, simply, without artificial assistance. I wanted to transcend the pure raw emotions of love and take them into some areas that were as yet unknown to me. After all, I was only nineteen. It seemed to me that the road stretched out long ahead of me, and that I had all the time in the world.

It was Cynthia who opened the door and asked me to come in. She was wearing a soft, pale, creamy sweater and a black skirt. She wore no make-up; her almost perfectly oval face looked mirror-like and austere.

"I'm so tired—*fatigué*," she said. "I worked all day long at the television studio with this stupid French director by the name of Roger. You know what he made me do? I had to stand on this platform and pretend to be a living doll—a *poupée*—and shake my head up and down, and back forth, and sing something silly, that ended with my saying '*Non, non, non, non, non.*' But I'm nobody's baby-doll, that's for sure!"

She boiled water and whisked some fragrant Japanese green tea. She handed it to me, then took off her sweater and folded it and crouched next to me, almost touching me with her pale bare shoulders, her slender hips, her willowy frame.

I felt no need to talk about myself or about anything and was just happy to be next to her and to share the meditative silence. I wondered how old she was; she could not have been more than twenty-one.

Was it Hemingway who had famously said, "If you are lucky enough to have lived in Paris as a young man, then whenever you go for the rest of your life it stays with you"?

Cynthia then looked so young and fine and fresh that next to her I felt like an old weathered lion. It disturbed me to think that I could possibly corrupt her and lead her astray with my burgeoning desire.

"I've been living with Pierre for a few months now," she said. "I like him, but it's nothing special. He's really good with a camera. He helped me put together my model portfolio after I gave up the flute. He's a really kind and sweet French guy, but he's got a lot of problems himself. He can't get work with the French fashion magazines because he insists on doing things his own way. Of course the editors can't accept that. And he's very short too, and that's maybe why he gets too aggressive in certain social situations. It makes me uncomfortable. So I stopped going out with him. I just share the apartment with him, we're like good pals."

"But it must be difficult, living with a guy like that, especially if you're sharing the same bed."

"No, I told him right away that I needed my own privacy, my own space around me, and that space was my right and inviolable. And he understood."

I wondered if these "privacy" rules would also extend to my relationship with her. But then I realized that I hardly knew her—that this was only the third time we had met (aside from the time when I had glimpsed her moving like a phantom down the long halls of the psych ward). Yet in some way I felt sure that I knew

her, that I had met her before, and that behind the silky modulations of her crystalline voice was hidden another voice that echoed a deeper part of myself and
brought back awesome memories.

"What are your hands shaking for? Are you not feeling well?" she asked me.

"No, sometimes I just get a little nervous, or over-excited."

"Have some more Japanese tea, it's very relaxing and good for you. It'll soothe
you and calm you down."

I sipped the delicate green tea slowly and watched her, wondering what her
next move would be. I knew that I desired her. The Paris afternoon, dappled with
late autumn warmth and sunlight, lay before us. But I did not wish to accelerate
my desire. I did not want to move toward any type of conclusion that might
break the spell of the moment. Cynthia had a presence that was as impossible to
describe—it was subtle, nuanced, and magical.

"I imagined when I first got here that Paris would be open and easy, and that
there would be many things I could do," she said, "but actually that wasn't the
case. Paris is a very hard city to live in. It's closed and cruel. You have to be lucky
to be able to get inside it and to feel its warmth and its very old soul."

"But did you come here just to study the flute?" I wondered.

"There's no exact reason why I came. It wasn't just for the flute. You know,
when I was a young girl, growing up in New Hampshire, I used to go to the
library and read Rimbaud. I loved that poet, he's so great—he invented a new
language, and then, having invented it, he turned away and did something else. I
believe he ended his life wandering around in Ethiopia … crazy … so maybe I
came to Paris because of Rimbaud, because I heard a little voice like a whisper
inside me which I trusted and followed. I've always trusted my instincts and feelings. How about you?"

She looked at me reading my eyes as if to get a quick confirmation that I was
on the same wave length. "Anyway, I don't know why I'm telling you these
things. I promise you I usually don't talk like this, but you got me talking."

I laughed. Then her look changed, became intense. She brought her smooth
oval face closer to my own, and she reached out and touched me, clasping me on
both sides of my head, squeezing a little and pressing against my forehead, as if
trying to reassure herself that I was truly there for her.

We were in a large, spacious photographer's studio with high ceilings and
white backdrops hung everywhere. An unmade bed near the entrance door bordered on the kitchen. The light poured in large sheets through the studio windows. It was an indolent, empty afternoon filled only with the strange promise of

our being together. It started and ended there. Nothing more happened between us. But I sensed that perhaps a promise had been given.

CHAPTER 9

▼

Through a classified ad in the *Herald-Tribune*, I managed to find a job at a French company called VIP Services. The job consisted of escorting visiting American businessmen around Paris. I met Allan Haller at 6 PM one evening in the Hemingway Bar at the Ritz Hotel. Allan at that time had been sent to Europe to represent the clothing line of the up-and-coming designer, Ralph Lauren. He was a flashy, self-made guy from Atlanta with a heavy southern accent who enjoyed flaunting his expense account. He wore expensive, pin-striped suits, gaudy ties, and shoes so buffed that you could have used them as shaving mirrors. While we were sipping Veuve Cliquot champagne at the Ritz bar, he noticed a tall, very attractive young woman who was seated at a nearby table with a rather obese Arab, traditionally dressed. Allan could not keep his eyes off of her. He asked me to go over to their table and deliver a note he had written on the back of his business card. While I was wondering how I would manage that, the Arab and the tall, sexy girl suddenly rose and left. Allan said, "Hey, I've got a new job for you. You know that Arab just didn't fit with that girl. I bet she's American and she's a model. She's sure got the looks. I think he's that famous arms dealer, Kashoggi something. Tell me this, how much are you making at VIP Services?"

I told him.

He said, "I'll pay you ten times that plus all your expenses. Here's your job: I want you to find that girl, her name, and track her down, and get her phone number. And when you do find her, I want you to play the first song on this tape I'm going to give you, it's "Pretty Woman" by Roy Orbison. You get yourself a tape player and you play this for her when you find her, and you tell her it's from me, from Allan Haller—okay, kid?"

Before I could answer he slapped me on the back, thrust a wad of hundred dollar bills into my hand, and said, "Don't call me until you have some results."

And so it was that I took a leave of absence from Paris and spent a week tracking Mr. Kashoggi and his American girlfriend Amanda down. When I finally caught up with Amanda, she was in a hospital in Rome recovering from some unexplained malady. I went into her hospital room and sat by her bed. She looked pale and exhausted and not nearly as good as she had that night at the Ritz. I told her that I had come on behalf of this American business guy, Allan Haller, and my mission was to play this tape for her. So we sat and listened to "Pretty Woman." It was corny and stupid, especially as she took it seriously, and said she was most interested in meeting Mr. Allan Haller. She said that she would be sure to call him as soon as she was feeling better. She asked me to lean over and kiss her, but I felt awkward about doing that, as in my mind she was already Allan Haller's property. And, besides, I was thinking about Cynthia.

But I had completed the mission, made some money, and had no use for Mr. Allan Haller any more. So that evening I flew back to Orly Airport. I always found it strange that you had to fill out little yellow arrival cards that asked your profession before they would let you through customs. What was my profession anyway? I put down "traveler" because I thought that was a good description of who I was. That's what I did—I traveled; I moved around.

It was a wind-tossed, pewter grey day. I collected my duffel bag and went outside and looked for a taxi. There was a lot of traffic going back into Paris. I told the cab driver to take a short cut at the porte d'Orléans. He shrugged his shoulders and gave me a dirty look. He was from North Africa, he said, had come to Paris with nothing, and he didn't like Americans. But I held firm. I was getting to know my way around. Soon we arrived at my "hole in the ground" at 9, rue Campagne-lrè.

It was quiet and dark inside. There was no mail. But in my underground dwelling I felt happier than I had ever been. When I thought back upon my days at St. Paul's School, and later the few months I had spent at Berkeley, I was amazed at how stupid and naïve I had been. I had imagined that the world belonged to me and that through some odd combination of drinks, drugs, and depression, I could possess it. But now I was in Paris on the verge of something new, and I no longer wanted anything to do with that older version of myself. I felt free of my imaginary prisons, ready to begin my real life.

CHAPTER 10

▼

I took a shower, changed my clothes, went out on the leafy boulevard Montparnasse, sat in one of the newer glass-enclosed cafés, and ordered a "*Petit-Crème*". Passers-by arose and disappeared before me, merging with the cropped trees, often led by those stupid little dogs Parisians were so fond of. For me, Paris was, above all, a vision and promised a sense of possibility. No one cared whether I was there, where I went, or what I did. The key point was to see how I could live with this new sense of freedom and, more importantly, how I could continue and maintain it.

It amused me to scribble down on the back of a napkin words that I thought might describe Cynthia: elusive, impulsive, unseizable, girl-spirited woman …

I was waiting for her at the Closerie des Lilas, the café on the corner where there was the statue of Napoleon's general with his raised sword, when she swooped down upon me.

We had a few *kir royales*. She was spunky, talkative, brimming with unusual stories. After the third or fourth drink, and while I was ordering fresh langoustines with mayonnaise and a bottle of chilled *Sancerre* for lunch, she suddenly leaned toward me and began to utter crazy, garbled words.

At first I didn't pay attention; I kept talking to the waiter, who deliberately played deaf and tried to get the lunch order straight.

Without warning, her head lolled against my shoulders. She seemed to half-choke, then lost consciousness, mumbling incoherently.

Two waiters helped me move her toward some empty seats on the leather *banquette*. There she lay in a deep sleep—a quasi-coma—with all the bubbling brouhaha and lunch-time agitation of the Closerie des Lilas around her.

I called a taxi and managed to get her inside, though the driver started cursing me, saying the taxi was where he "lived," and he didn't want a sick young woman in his "home."

Then I took Cynthia back to my cellar studio at 9, rue Campagne-lrè and laid her on the narrow bed. She lay perfectly still, with a slight smile on her face, and she looked child-like and happy. I remembered our meeting in the corridor of the psychiatric ward and the quick, rapid-fire exchange of glances and gestures. Later, there were the lilting sounds of her silver flute wafting in through the thick, barred windows. That had been her way of sending a message to me, of saying, *I am here, don't despair, we will meet again for sure.* Her long, blonde hair framed her lovely face and I stood looking at her with concern. I thought she might be more comfortable if I removed some of her clothes, but she cried softly, "No, no, just leave me alone." And so I left her alone, lying fully clothed across my bed. I lit a candle and sat on a chair next to the bed watching over her with anxious longing.

Her parents, she said, had sent her to that psychiatric hospital because they did not know how to deal with her. They were simple people from a paper mill town and they had hoped she would do well in high school and conform to their expectations. But she had a wild, impetuous nature and longed to escape the narrow, conservative bounds in which she had grown up. Once, when she was invited to a dance at a preppy boarding school, it was rumored she had had an "escapade" with the class guitar player, who was subsequently expelled. At the insistence of her parents, she had agreed to attend a "summer session" at the psychiatric hospital. She agreed only because she thought: *Afterwards, I will be free, or I will know how to find my freedom.* And when I met her there by accident, I knew at once, recognized at once, that she had in her that essential trembling flicker, that little but vital spark of freedom, of desire to be master of herself and her own destiny, that would later lead her to so many strange places and extraordinary adventures. And, as she later told me, "Instead of just talking, I did."

It was 1966. The wild sixties were just getting underway—that decade of imagination let loose, of revolt and sensuality and new music and liberation. Looking back, it is hard for me not to think of how stupid and naïve I was then, but perhaps no more so than the youth of any other generation, to dare to imagine that the world belonged to us, or could be transformed and made to belong to us, and that by acts of love and poetry and violence we could possess it, the magic of love, and make it our own.

Cynthia awoke with a start shortly after midnight. "Oh my God, what happened to me? I don't believe it! Pierre will never forgive me! I've got to get home."

I held her and accompanied her outside down the dark rue Campagne-lrè to the traffic light at the corner of the boulevard Raspail. It was good to breathe the clear, cold Paris autumnal air. There was hardly any traffic. The night was bottomless and black. She noticed the quality of it and said, "What a lot if silence there is. And look how funny those little cars look."

I flagged a cab. She lifted her face toward me, and I wanted to grab her in my arms and hold on to her, but I knew I could not do that; it was not yet the right time or moment.

"What happened to me?" she wondered. "I just don't understand. I must have gone crazy, being with you. I must have just lost it, how weird!"

I held her close to me and kissed her quickly on the lips. The night air brushed between us. There was a large gaping silence. "Whatever happens," I said. "Whatever happens."

She nodded and ducked into the cab and was gone.

That was not the last time I saw her in a state of unconsciousness. I quickly realized there was that in her nature which was fragile and volatile, which at any moment, for unknown reasons, could shatter like quicksilver into hundreds of pieces.

Was I like that myself? I wondered. Was that why I felt myself drawn so powerfully to her? Because she held up a mirror to my own unstable and dangerous nature? The doctors who had interviewed me at the hospital had questioned my need for evasion, for flight—my need to create distances. And essentially it was because I could not trust anyone, and in fact, had no one to trust. The betrayal that had occurred when they had forced a straitjacket on me and locked me in a barred room with a tiny grilled window in the metal door so the nurses could look in on me, and with the straps on the bed tying down my arms and legs so that I could not move, was the last indignity. I had vowed to myself that, once I escaped from that hospital, I would never let anyone get close enough to me to put me in that kind of danger again. Was that, then, why I was drawn to the bright-spirited but evasive and elusive Cynthia? I didn't know, but I knew I had to find out.

During the early days in Paris, when I lived on practically nothing, surviving on bread and wine and cheese, speaking to no one, assuming a total solitude, I learned the power and energy that came from that feeling of control. And I learned better how to control my own demonic forces—with one fatal exception, the force and longing of sex.

Late at night I would often go out wandering in the streets of Paris, hoping to get lost, looking everywhere for a voice, a familiar face, a recognition in whatever form. I would wander for hours, sometimes until the early morning when African street sweepers appeared with their long brooms. I would stop on one of the many beautiful bridges over the Seine and stand looking for a long time at the reflections in the dark restless waters below.

Sometimes I went as far as Les Halles, the old central market area, where you could see the slabs of meat carcasses and the butchers in their bloody white uniforms. The prostitutes on rue St. Denis would beckon to me from shadowy doorways, and there was one I was particularly attracted to, who always dressed in black, and had ample, overflowing breasts and particularly wide hips. I didn't have quite enough francs, but she told me that, if I would go buy her a big basket of *frites,* she would go with me, so I came back with the french fries overflowing out of the basket, and when she saw them, she turned and started climbing the narrow stairs. Watching her monumental buttocks sway, and with the *frites* falling out of the paper cone, I mounted behind her, panting like a dog with breathlessness and hope.

Cynthia had told me that her relationship with Pierre was "brotherly at best." Still, days would go by without my getting a chance to see her. I felt she was deliberately keeping a certain distance between us. She knew she could not always control herself. In some way she was afraid of what might happen between us if all the forces were truly let loose.

I would take day trips to the countryside. I spent five days at Chartres in the shadow of the great cathedral. I liked the idea of motion, of mobility—it suited my inner restlessness. It helped strengthen me in my thinking that there was really no reason to call any particular place home.

Once I went out walking very early in the Luxembourg Gardens. I saw the dawn breaking, the light swooping down in broad bands over the plane trees. Clear water gurgled in the basins of the horse-proud fountains. I felt good in my heart, clear and strong. From now on I would proceed in my life without compromises. My heart was at peace. Even loneliness felt keen and sharp, like a friendly sword that sustained me. At that moment, I wondered if I needed Cynthia or any woman. What, after all, could she bring to me? Was it just the illusion of the golden triangle of sexual fulfillment? But I knew what that was; I had already tried it many times. So certainly it must have been something else—what exactly I did not know, but again I had a strong instinctive feeling that here in Paris at last I would find it.

CHAPTER 11

▼

Her name was Ode. She came from the mountains of Morocco. She had arrived in Paris without anything and had gotten work doing some photo shoots for fashion magazines because she was tall and striking, with full breasts but thin hips and strong almost masculine thighs. She would strut forward with her shoulders back, her long jet-black hair streaming behind her, and it was impossible not to look at her.

I don't remember how she had met Cynthia, but I could tell at once from the way they talked and laughed and shared together that they were best friends.

At a wild summer party at a private house in Neuilly, she had met Maurice P.—the well-known French playwright. He was older and married to a society woman, and, although they led separate lives and had a supposedly "open marriage," Maurice insisted on the utmost discretion. In Paris, everyone talks, and he did not want anyone to be able to talk about him or what he did or whom he saw. So he instructed Ode that, if she wanted to be with him, whenever they saw each other, they could never speak, only make signs from a distance with their hands, with their bodies. Ode said that suited her fine, because she did not like or trust words anyway. She had grown up in the mountains among sheep and chicken and goats, and, even when she and Maurice were together, she much preferred to act out their fantasies with her body, saying nothing.

"Ode's a beautiful woman," said Cynthia. "And I love her name, don't you? Do you know what it means?"

"No, what?"

"In German, it means emptiness, the void, the desert. And she's just like that, she creates this feeling of desert space around her, you can just feel it."

We decided we would take a trip together. It would be Cynthia and Pierre and Ode and me.

"Where should we go? There are so many places!" Ode wondered.

"I love going to the train stations here," I said, "like the gare d'Austerlitz. I sit down and watch the trains come and go, and sometimes I play 'train roulette' and jump on the first train that's going anywhere. I go with that train to the first stop and then come back."

It was Cynthia who suggested we drive to Normandy "to sense the ocean."

So, one misty, rainy Saturday we piled into Pierre's old Citroen—a *deux chevaux*—but after we got to Rouen it broke down, so we had to spend most of the night inside a desolate garage while an illiterate mechanic pried open the hood and tried to fix the car and couldn't.

Somehow, Ode got talking with a French farmer who had stopped for gas, and he picked us up and took us to his farmhouse where he proudly showed us his goats and then his basement where he had stored thousands of bottles of calvados. The next day we took the train from Rouen to Deauville and we walked along the boardwalk and "sensed the ocean." There was a brisk wind blowing in. It was cold, there was almost no one there, and Ode said she liked the empty spaces and would like to have a house on a cliff overlooking the sea. Cynthia walked ahead with Pierre, just holding his hand lightly, and I wondered if they were truly together or not, and finally decided it didn't matter, because, if it was my fate to be with her, then that would surely happen.

We took the late afternoon train back from Deauville to Paris. A few days later, Ode went to the American Hospital of Paris where she got a job washing down cadavers, cleaning them for burial.

"Why did you do that?" I wondered. "There are other ways of making money in Paris, I've done it myself."

"You know, I have to tell you," she said. "Being alone never scared me. But I've never been able to get over my fear of death. So I thought if I could go to the hospital and get a job washing corpses, that's as close to death as I could possibly get. And, little by little, I would lose my fear, so even death would cease to have any meaning for me."

Ode's relationship with Maurice did not last long. "None of my relationships last long," she told Cynthia. "I'm so tired of having men see me and they all have this idea of me, which is of something exotic and strange because of the way I look, and, of course, I am Moroccan, and they feel this need to possess me, and, once they do, then often they are not so interested, because I was just there for them—one moment in time, one exotic fleeing image …"

"But what is your idea of love then?" I enquired, "if you can't be with any man for any length of time."

She grasped Cynthia's hand. "Listen, my dear, let me tell you the most important thing I've learned: if you are truly interested in a certain idea of love that is free of compromises—and for me love must be free of compromises or it quickly becomes a bondage/dependency situation and for me that's not love—then you can never spend more than three nights with a man. I've tested this many times: one night and two nights, but three nights is the absolute limit. Yes, remember that, dear Cynthia: three nights is the absolute maximum that you can sleep with someone if you want to keep the intensity and purity and absolute nature of the physical passion."

Cynthia was quick to adopt this idea she got from Ode of the "law of three nights." She was very fond of it and often repeated it. Since I still had not succeeded in even spending one night with her, I teased Cynthia and said, "How about if I trade three for one?"

"*Pazienza*," she said in Italian. "It takes time. And maybe your time will come!"

Cynthia began going out with Ode more and more often. I was angry with Ode because I felt she was taking Cynthia away from me, and ultimately I could not agree with her ideas about love and solitude and the "law of three nights." Ode was a true loner, and yet she used Cynthia as a support. Also, Ode liked to have the feeling that she could dominate men or subjugate them with the power of her physical presence, and I did not go for that. I simply did not feel attracted to her. And she knew it and resented it.

Ode's long silences, her austerity, her indifferent aloofness, troubled me. Still, as Ode had become so close to Cynthia, I welcomed the chances I had to be with her, as I felt that, through Ode, I could find out more about Cynthia.

So I would often go with Ode on long random walks along the banks of the Seine in the early evenings, sometimes sitting down on the stone steps with the *clochards*—the bums, the down-and-outers. We would watch the Paris lights shining off the clear, cold, dark waters near the Pont Neuf.

One of Ode's favorite things was smoking marijuana. There were many friends who always seemed to be arriving with fresh supplies from Casablanca or Tangiers. She rolled them herself, of course, and whenever she lit one up, she would smile broadly and pass it around, an open invitation.

"Want to try a drag?" Cynthia said.

When she had first come to Paris, she told me, she had smoked one night by herself. But she took too much, and it knocked her out—bango, down and out!

She looked at me with that pale, mysterious smile that always seemed to say and promise more than it did.

"Never smoke by yourself," Ode cautioned me. "Because you never know how far you're going, or when you'll hit your limits."

Ode was fascinated by death. She said that, by getting close by death, by washing dead bodies, she felt that she was that much closer to life.

"I was always so afraid of it," she told Cynthia. "And I couldn't live with this fear any more. Now it means nothing to me. And it really is nothing, believe me—I've seen so many corpses!"

Ode would share with us her strong feeling that a new apocalypse was about to happen. All the signs, both astrological and geological, pointed toward it. The first warnings would come in the form of some gigantic natural disturbance, like an earthquake or some radical climate change. If you wanted to be on the cutting edge of this new upheaval, California was the place to be. "That's where it's all going to start," Ode said. "I'm trying to get enough money together to go there."

Cynthia was quick to agree. "I understand completely," she said. "You want to be there in the new space just before it happens, to get as close to the decisive event as possible."

"Yes," said Ode, inhaling deeply. "We are now living the fourth cycle of human evolution. It's the last one. The best we can do is to be a good witness."

I didn't bother to ask Ode what the other three cycles were, or if the first cycle was a bicycle, the second one a car, the third one a plane, the fourth a space ship, etc. To tell the truth, I didn't really like Ode or trust her. It disturbed me that she kept trying to seduce Cynthia into accepting her ideas about the fleeting nature of love and "the law of three nights." I guess I wasn't naïve enough to think that the world, ever since it began, had not been living a bloody tragedy. I felt that Ode's uncompromising attitude, her furious emphasis on freedom at all costs—I can still hear her saying, "After three nights even the most intense passionate love affair inevitably becomes a history of compromise"—prevented her from having any real relationship with a man—or with a woman, for that matter. And I told her so.

As if to retaliate against me, Ode began going out more and more with Cynthia. She asked me to come along, but I declined, because I didn't want to encourage their camaraderie, and I felt that Cynthia would soon grow tired of the relationship. Yet my antipathy toward Ode only seemed to strengthen Cynthia's resolve to befriend her and accompany her.

One afternoon, with the tarnished silver light falling on the trees and statues in the Tuileries garden, Cynthia paused in the middle of our promenade and asked, "Tell me, what have you got against Ode? Why are you so irritated and upset every time I go out with her?"

I hesitated, not quite knowing how to answer.

"Isn't Ode a free spirit?" she pursued.

"Yes, she's a free spirit for sure."

Actually, I knew that if it had not been for my own desire for Cynthia—to possess what was not yet mine—I might have more easily accepted Ode, because I felt somehow that she had succeeded in obtaining access to an intimate part of Cynthia that was still closed to me.

"You know," Cynthia said, "at bottom, I think you're afraid of Ode. She's too strong a woman. She's not going to yield to any man and that makes you afraid, poor you."

"Look," I replied angrily. "That's not it at all! You really want to know? Well, here it is: Ode drags around too much, and she's always smoking something, wanting to get high. Basically, she's a nomad, a gypsy. One day she's here, tomorrow she disappears for three nights or three years, who knows? Cynthia, I'm sorry, but I just can't deal with that, and I don't want you to either."

We sat down on one of the stone benches. It was a cold steel-bright day in early December. I looked up at the chimney-potted roofs that lined rue de Rivoli. The golden statue of Joan of Arc surged a short distance in front of us.

"How can I make you understand?" Cynthia said. "It's just that I feel good when I'm with Ode. I like to share a little green tea with her, smoke a little bit, feel calm and happy."

That made me angry. I had been to one of Ode's famous "green tea parties." Ode had talked about her life in the desert, about how she had traveled with the "blue men" on their camels.

I said, "I went to one of her parties. All she wanted to do was tell her Moroccan stories, make hashish crepes, and smoke grass! That's all, that's it. There are so many other ways to get high."

"No, absolutely not, I don't agree," Cynthia said. "In the West there are so few ways of getting to heaven or getting high as you say. And the ways that are provided are so limited and artificial. Why not smoke grass anyway? It's not hard drugs, after all. Just because you take a tote now and then, doesn't mean you're an addict—no more than the fact that you drink a few glasses of white wine means you're an alcoholic."

"Perhaps," I said. "But the fact is, your friend Ode really smokes a lot."

"Hah! It just bothers you that she smokes more and enjoys it more than you!"

"Not only that," I said, "but Ode doesn't like anyone to talk. She just sits there, smiling and looking at you."

"Of course not! Who wants to talk when you're feeling so good? Remember this: the true and good and beautiful things can never be said. We know them and we feel them, that's all."

I was silent. Was Cynthia right? Was it wrong to wish to enter a state of quiet serenity and bliss?

"So Ode smokes," Cynthia continued. "So what? *Et alors?* Smoking grass clears up your mind. It puts a good head on your shoulders. It makes you objective. You know, if you smoked more, you'd probably feel better yourself!"

"I doubt it," I said quickly. "I'd feel impersonal, detached—exactly the opposite of how I want to feel."

"And how do you want to feel?"

"I want to feel the crazy flow of things, not just sit there, numb and impassive!"

"Oh, you're so wrong. Smoking is the very opposite of making you impersonal. You know, you don't just go 'pammo' and collapse. On the contrary, you sit up, become calm, relaxed and lucid, capable of really participating in a new way."

We had approached the Seine. We were walking near the place du Chatelet, across the busy bridge that connects to the Île de la Cité where the flower market and bird market were.

Beneath us the Bateaux Mouches excursion boats floated by, crowded with tourists greedily trying to grasp as much of the fleeting beauty of Paris as they could.

We sat down at a café across from the soaring spire of that gothic church, the Sainte-Chapelle, with the sacred stained glass windows. I ordered two *petits-crèmes* and a *baguette fromage*. Cynthia looked at me with her bright, blue, challenging eyes.

"I just don't feel comfortable with that lifestyle," I said. "I'm trying to have a relationship with you, and Ode keeps interrupting it. She's the stranger that comes in a whirlwind and leaves ruin and destruction in her wake. Haven't you noticed how nothing is ever the same after she's been with us?"

"Listen," she insisted. "Ode's a new, a very modern woman. I think she's great. She's got so many real, true things inside her. I think what scares you about her is just her freedom, her independence from men. Tell me now, isn't that so?"

Her defense of her friend hurt me.

"Okay, if you so much want to be independent, just go and be that way!" I exclaimed. "Just don't come see me any more!"

"Look," she answered, angry now, "people are just not submitting themselves to anyone any more. That's all gone, baby. The woman no longer just stays in the house, in case you haven't figured that out. If you're going to expect me to do that, you're out of your mind. I've got to have a life of my own! Ode's my friend. *Viva Ode!*"

As if to prove her point, Cynthia disappeared for a few days.

I had no idea where she had gone. She had always had that impulsive side to her. Her parents had sent her to the mental institution where I was briefly confined because they were worried about all her artistic activities outside of school. I, too, had left many things behind, often at a moment's notice, so I could fully understand how she used the "art of the flight" as a refuge, a way of finding her balance. Still, I was worried because I had no idea when she was going to come back. I figured that if anyone knew, it was probably Ode. So I gave in and called Ode.

She agreed to meet me late one afternoon in the gardens of the Palais Royal. That was where Colette and Jean Cocteau had lived, and I felt I could still feel their spirits. We walked slowly up and down the long sandy paths.

"I had a big argument with Cynthia," I told Ode. "I was just beginning to get close to her. And then she just up and left. I think she left like that to spite me. Her absence is a test, a provocation, don't you think?"

Ode smiled. "I know you like Cynthia very much. And why shouldn't you? She's beautiful, and she has this mysterious life-spark that everyone feels. But you must be careful. For she is very young and is still looking for who she is—her real identity. If she is lucky, she will find it. Perhaps you will help her to find it. *Que sais-je?* I don't know. But remember, she has not yet had the really strong experience that will make her definitively into something. She is waiting here in Paris for something fantastic to happen. She has her future ahead of her. You know more than she does. You must be careful not to hurt her, or to let her hurt you by, how shall I say, certain of her innocent or careless actions."

Ode's comments made me smile with wry bitterness. It was ridiculous—strolling up and down in that superb symmetrical garden, talking so seriously about someone who wasn't even there, and who perhaps could not have cared less. What I knew then was that I did not know very much about Cynthia. And did it matter? I had come to Paris in search of something, to live an adventure. It was only this "now" that was important. What had happened yesterday, what might happen tomorrow, did not matter.

Ode leaned against one of the columns that bordered the alleys flanked with bright flowerbeds. "I am not afraid of anything," she said. "That is my personal lesson, what I had to learn. That is why I go every day to the American Hospital to wash and clean dead bodies before they are cremated or buried. This is what Cynthia must learn. It may be a different knowledge, but it will come from the same source. She must find what she is most afraid of, and then she must live that."

"But how many of those bodies do you have to wash before you're no longer afraid? And after that, then what are you going to do?"

She shrugged. She was wearing a necklace of heavy amber beads that she said she had gotten from a trader at the camel market in Tiznit. "I don't know. Who knows? *Qui sait? Qui peut savoir?* What can anyone know anyway? Perhaps I will go back to the desert in Morocco. You know, I come from a very simple town. We raised goats and chickens. I feel strangely at peace when I am in the desert. I might want to live there again. Maybe I will marry one of those 'Blue Men,' a 'Touareg,' one of those warriors of the desert who travel back and forth with their camels, carrying everything they own with them, not caring at all for the future. It could be a beautiful life, no? No future, no cares, no worries, so simple!"

In silence we walked back across the cool stone bridges, past the grand gargoyled towers of Notre Dame, alone in Paris, city of exiles, of hope, and light.

CHAPTER 12

▼

I was alone in my basement studio late one night when I heard an insistent scratching at the window. Cynthia was outside on the sidewalk. I opened the window and looked up at her.

"Where in the hell have you been?" I yelled.

"I'm all right," she answered quietly. It was all she would say. She just kept saying, "I'm okay, I'm all right."

It was painful to listen to her laconic, almost indifferent replies. Old feelings I could not deny came back and pounded away in my mind.

"Were you with a man?" I pushed for an answer, some clue.

"No."

"A woman?" I asked ironically, thinking of Ode.

"I'm not going to answer that," she said.

But later she said, "It's funny you asked me about being with a woman. Because I do feel attracted to Ode. But it's more her way of thinking that attracts me—you know, her 'desert sand' philosophy. Sometimes I wish I could be like her—a free spirit! I don't want to possess anything ... no heavy baggage. What a burden!"

"But even a free spirit must live in a body," I tried to reason with her.

"Yes," she laughed in her crystalline way, "but you just say that, like all the other men, because you just want to sleep with me!"

"And if I did, what would be so wrong with that? You must know by now that I have feelings for you—that for a long time I've had this crazy desire for you."

She was silent for a moment, picked up her silver flute, piped some wistful notes. "Remember what my friend Ode says—you cannot sleep with a man for more than three nights because, if you do, you will ruin the purity of that passion. And that's what's beautiful between us—the purity and fineness of that passion. If I slept with you, it would finish it; it would become banal, ordinary, and I wouldn't be able to see you again. And I like you, and want to see you, and that is why it is better that we only make love to each other by talking and not touching. Besides," she added, "I do live with Pierre, and, even though he and I are like brother and sister, he gets very jealous; he doesn't want me sleeping with anyone."

"But are you sleeping with Pierre?" I had to know.

She laughed mockingly, explosively. "And why should I tell you whether I am sleeping with Pierre? What possible difference does it make? Is that the only thing you are worried about? Yes, I already told you, I like Pierre, he's a superb photographer, he takes great pictures of me, but he's too jealous, and I don't like jealousy or possessiveness. That's exactly what I want to free myself of ... all those chains!"

That evening ended as so many others had, with no conclusion. I put her in a cab at the corner of the boulevard Raspail and rue Campagne-lrè and watched as she disappeared down the long rain-streaked, glistening boulevard to the apartment she shared with Pierre near the Jardin des Plantes. I went to the Rosebud, a smoky intimate bar I knew on rue Delambre where I had a few Carlsberg beers and flirted for the sake of form with the local *fashionettes*. Then I walked back to my "hole in the ground" at 9, rue Campagne-lrè and went to bed, thinking of Ode and Cynthia, of my grandmother a long time ago, of loves lost and regained, of Paris, and of the sad, fleeting nature of all things.

The money I had was rapidly running out. I was in a state of anxiety wondering how many odd jobs I would be able to do or find. It was true that money was not important to me. Still, I had to live, and I didn't want to be forced for financial reasons to return to the States. So it was an unexpected blessing when a letter arrived from my grandmother. She wrote that her old Scottish cook Molly had just died. She said that, although she had been against it, she now understood that it was important for me to stay in Paris, to live my life—*vivre ma vie*. She was going to start sending me every month a small sum, part of the money she used to give Molly. "Money's like manure," she added. "If you don't throw it around, the wild flowers never get a chance to grow." I kissed the envelope. I still have it. It bought me time and freedom.

When Cynthia was not working on her photo shoots for *Vogue* magazine or *Le Journal des Modes*, she would stop by to see me unexpectedly, often knocking at my window from the outside. We would go walking together down the long shaded alleys of the Luxembourg Gardens. Sometimes she brought me haunting meditative music that I had not heard before and told me I had to learn how to be quiet and to still my mind.

Cynthia would sit with her knees crossed in a yoga-like position in the shadows of my little room. I would light a candle and some incense, the music would flow, sometimes she played her silver flute, we talked about magic and drugs and voyages. Sometimes she would even lie next to me, but, if I moved to touch her, she would gently move my hands away.

"Let's just pretend that we're like brother and sister," she urged. "So we can lie with each other and be friendly, just touching, but no more than touching—not now, not yet."

I felt I didn't need drugs to get high, and I could do without the illusions of magic, but what about the power of sex? *El Poder del Sexo?* How could I accept to live without that when it was so much inside me and part of my intimate structure, my heart and flesh and brain?

Cynthia lay on the bed with all the sounds of the Paris streets and the Paris night rushing just beyond the half-shuttered window. The light flickered across her lovely oval, face. She lay propped on her elbows, just looking at me. She drew up her legs, her back slightly arched. I touched her soft, baby-blue sweater. I inserted my hand under it and started to caress her pert firm breasts. She did not move. I wondered how far she would let me go. But as I started to press against her, she stopped me and pulled back.

"I want to tell you about myself," she said. "You really know nothing about me. You have just met me in Paris and decided that, because you are in Paris and bored and alone, you will love me, and, because you are used to getting what you want, you should have me."

"No, I'm not bored—absolutely, not at all," I answered. "No, it's not like that, not at all!

Cynthia laughed suddenly, in bright, expanding, crystalline waves. She tossed her long hair back and sat up and straightened her legs. Then she kneeled and assumed a sphinx-like position.

"I'm here in Paris to forget my past," she said. "But I will tell you a little bit."

CHAPTER 13

▼

There was a time, she told me, when life had seemed so clear, easy, and straight-forward! She had been living on a communal farm called The Golden Age not far from the University of New Hampshire. It was there that she had met Phil, an editor of underground newspapers. Phil and his friends had introduced her to new ways of thinking and feeling that were non-linear and non-possessive and nature-oriented. Cynthia had read old Buddhist scriptures and written down:

> *I want to think.*
> *You cannot think without faith.*
> *How can I get faith?*
> *You cannot get faith without action.*
> *How to learn to act?*
> *Be happy!*

But her father—a simple man who had spent his life working in a paper mill—had developed some rare blood disease. Her family's small resources were soon devoted to taking care of medical bills. Cynthia had to take a typing job at a nearby automobile parts factory. It was not a very active or creative task, the daily punching in of thousands of numbers. It was not healthy for her; she felt she was "going nuts." She had no car, and on cold winter days she had to walk back and forth three or four miles to and from work. Then Phil showed up one morning and said he had really good news: he had just been offered an important new job as editor of an underground paper in San Francisco, and was driving across coun-try immediately. Can I come with you? Cynthia had asked. She was ready to leave. But Phil said no, he couldn't take her with him, he had to go alone, but he very much wanted to give her a farewell present: a one-way ticket to Paris on Icelandic airlines. "Don't be afraid to live your dreams," he told her.

When Cynthia arrived in Paris, she lived in a succession of small hotels. But as her mother was French-Canadian, she spoke French fluently. And, since she was young, vivacious, and attractive, it was easy for her to meet French people in the teeming café life around the ancient church St-Germain-des-Prés. She met writers and artists and photographers, and finally Pierre, who invited her to do some photo shoots with him. A four-page spread entitled "The Many Masks of Cynthia" soon appeared in a fashion magazine. In those photos, artfully staged, Cynthia assumed various feminine personas, such as the vamp, the sprite, the seductress, the clown, the little lost girl, the up-and-coming business woman, etc. This series of photos made her a sudden success. Photographers vied with each other to use her.

"She is so plastic, she can become anything," said a fashion editor. "It's as if she has no self and instantaneously adapts to whatever 'self' you want her to be."

But Cynthia was not happy with her photo career and soon grew tired of the constant and rigorous demands of modeling.

"And I couldn't deal with all these French and Italian men coming after me," she said. "I got to feel I was like a pack of gum and they all just wanted a stick."

It was at that fateful juncture that, by total chance, I had met her one afternoon at the American Express office as I was going to get my mail.

It was true that I had never met anyone quite like Cynthia. And it wasn't just the fact that I had not yet been able to possess her that intrigued me and kept me interested.

One of her girlfriends put it this way: "When you see her, you don't forget her. Why? Because you can't define her. You look at her, like at some moving light, and you think, there she is, that's her, that's what she is, but no it isn't, she's already moved on, danced on, become something else. She's like one of those mythical water spirits, so spontaneous, ever-changing, and completely unpredictable, of course!"

Even though I was not without knowing that she also had a mad, prophetic side, I still felt that she was my destined *amor* and *fata desiderata*—love and destined fate—the other side of the mirror I had come to Paris to find.

"How are you? Tell me, are you all right?" Cynthia was asking with a note of urgency. "I had the most terrible dream about you. I was lying in bed and you came walking through the window toward me. Except you were a ghost and you had been decapitated."

"Right," I said, "that's how I feel these days, like I've lost my head."

"I just wanted to tell you that ... I'm afraid something strange and fearful is going to happen to you, if it hasn't already."

"No, I'm okay," I said. "I've still got my head on. I'm just trying to get used to this wonderful feeling of being alone in Paris and not having any fixed obligations. How long can it last?"

"Don't ask that question. It's always a mistake."

There was silence. I wanted to reach out and try to hold her in that moment. But she spun away quickly.

"Right. You're in Paris. No one knows you. No one knows me. We're alone. We can do whatever we want. We can go as high as we want. There's no limit to how high or how far we can go. So let's just try to go higher, higher, higher ..."

"Hey, I've got a new name for you," I teased. "Your Royal Highness."

"Haha! Very funny, Mr.—!"

Later she would tell me, "I don't want you ever to tell anyone about me or to ever use my name. Just think of me as an anonymous female friend, an androgynous spirit locked up in the bottle of a woman's body!"

But I could not think of her without a name, she was always Cynthia to me— *Cinzia* as her Italian friends called her—and I could not reduce her to the abstract sylph-like essence she said she wanted to be.

As I came to know her over those days and weeks, as little by little she revealed herself to me, I grew afraid for her. I sensed there were so many abysses stretched beneath her. She had been rescued from them once, but it would be ever so easy for her to trip into them again.

Cynthia did not make it easy for me to see her. Between her modeling work and her various rendezvous, she was constantly busy. Whenever we did get to a café in St. Germain or Montparnasse, she was always quickly recognized. Friends from different countries, of both sexes, were always coming up to her, kissing her warmly in the French way on both cheeks, and sharing the latest Paris information with her. It was strange to think that she, an unknown young American girl, had come to know so many French people in such a short time. I found the French hard to talk to and often rude. That wasn't the case for her, and it only increased my desire to know her more and—finally—to become one with her and, in my fantasy, to take her away to some paradise island of *luxe, calme et volupté*, where we would not be hassled or bothered, and I would not have to share her with so many pressing admirers.

But it was clear I was getting nowhere with her, and I would wonder at times, in such a hopeless case, if there was any hope at all to be found. That bitter sense of primordial solitude I had always felt returned to me. I knew animal fear, a kind of loathing and self-disgust. To continue, I had to find a way to go beyond the tight circle of thoughts and words. I wanted to reach out and embrace a fullness, a totality—but where, and how to do that? How to achieve that transcendence, that legendary "breaking through to the other side"?

CHAPTER 14

▼

We were about two hours outside of Paris, on a farm in a Normandy village. Cynthia had asked Ode and myself if we wanted to accompany her on a photo shoot to see her *au boulot* (at work). She was dressed to the nines in a white lace dress, her lustrous blonde hair swept back. Her job was to stand flirtatiously in the middle of a cow field, her eyes fixed on a French farmer garbed as an American cowboy, shooting a big black revolver at a target of a blown-up camembert cheese. It was absurd to think that the image of the American West combined with a sensuous young woman and the inflated "cheese" would appeal to anyone. Ode said it was very French. The grass was high and thick where Cynthia stood, and the farmer kept wanting to pop his gun before he was given the signal. They had to redo the scene many times. Afterwards, the farmer invited everyone back to his farmhouse where he served some fruity red wine.

In the fall, he said, he had a part-time job hunting wild game. He loved animals, he assured us, but his real work was to hunt them down and kill them—especially the deer in the forests of Fontainbleau.

On the auto-route back to Paris, there was an accident involving a Mercedes that, at high speed, had swerved across the median and collided with a truck carrying a load of potatoes. A monstrous traffic jam resulted. Frustrated drivers lay on their horns. Potatoes were spilled all over the road. There was nothing to do but wait.

Cynthia turned to Ode in the back seat. "You know that big farmer guy who was shooting the gun? Well, I just had this strange fantasy about making love with him."

"Why would you do that?" I said sharply. "You didn't even seem to like him."

"Yes, but I was thinking I'd like to see what it feels like to make love to such a big guy who kills animals for a living."

"Yes," Ode chimed in, "that's exactly how I think, too. One must be able to make love without any feeling or attachment."

A pause. "And why is that?" I challenged her. "How can you just want to do away with any idea of love or romance or feeling?"

"You really want to know?" she responded with her broad ironic smile. "It's because we have no future. The future means nothing at all. So then why bother getting attached to anything or anyone?"

"But then there's no possible happiness," I said. "There's just the void, the blank space of every day—the desert."

The auto-route had been cleared, the traffic started to move. Cynthia glanced around. "What is this idea of happiness anyway?" she said. "What is it really? Just an idea—it's not real, it's an abstraction, a concept, a *promesse*, as the French say."

"Right on," Ode continued. "The moment you live a moment of happiness, it disappears and it leaves behind it always the desire for a new and unreachable happiness."

"Just like those dogs racing after the rabbit, round and round they go, never getting it," Cynthia quickly agreed.

"All these ideas! All these words! What a lot of bullshit!" I laughed. Later, when I was safely ensconced in my "hole in the ground" on rue Campagne-lrè, I was still smiling with contemptuous amusement at myself, thinking how easy it was to get caught up in this stream of feelings and thoughts—all because I was horny, beset with desire and fascination for this young woman. It would no doubt all end so quickly if I could just have an old-fashioned roll in the hay with her. I hadn't been able to do that yet, so it remained out there, a challenge and lure. Meanwhile, as they always do, the days went by inexorably, tinted by the tarnished silver gray light of Paris.

I won't be able to leave, I thought, until I've settled this mind-body-love thing with Cynthia.

CHAPTER 15

▼

"There's a birthday party for me tomorrow night," Cynthia called. "All my friends will be there. I want you to come. It's *chez* my friend Barbara. 10 PM. Don't be late, okay?"

"How many years?"

"Oh, I'm old," she said. "I'm an old soul."

"How old?"

"Twenty," she said.

I was not late. In fact, I was the first to arrive. There was an opened bottle of Dom Perignon on the table and numerous elegant hors d'oeuvres. The music of the great guitar player Django Rheinardt could be heard in the background. The penthouse apartment on the quai des Grands-Augustins, overlooking the Notre-Dame cathedral, belonged to Barbara, a wealthy poetess from New York City whose husband, an investment banker, was notably absent. Cynthia greeted me warmly, as if I were one of her oldest friends, embracing and kissing me on both cheeks. "I'm so happy you came. I don't go to parties often but this is special because it's my birthday and many of my good friends will be here. I know when we were coming back from Normandy that day, you said you really wanted to have some alone time with me. Well, we'll do that soon, I promise you. Tonight I just want you to meet my friends. Okay? *Ça va?*"

"Yes," I said warily. Because what else could I say? I was just happy to be there. A tray of champagne glasses floated by. I grabbed one.

In the corner I could see Ode. She was wearing a royal blue *djellaba*. She had a bright scarf around her head, and I was stunned to see that she had shaved her head. She was virtually bald. She looked like one of those Nubian warrior women. Why had she engaged in such a radical gesture, I wondered. To flaunt her freedom? Her self-avowed independence, her proud aloofness? What I knew was that I wanted Cynthia for myself, and I needed to keep her away from Ode.

That night, amid the dizzying clink of glasses and sparkling euphoria of all the international guests, I sensed that Cynthia, for the first time, was looking at me in a special, quasi-possessive way. She winked at me and squeezed my hand and smiled at my jokes. It seemed she was going out of her way to make me feel that I was special to her, and that she was offering me—or going to offer me—something secret, unique, and different.

Ode turned to her companion. "I cut my hair because I wanted to reduce myself to the barest essence," I heard her saying.

Other guests continued to arrive. Outside, on the balcony, with a view dominating the shiny dark waters of the Seine, you could see in close-up, almost as if you could reach out and touch them, the massive twin towers of Notre Dame.

"What do you think about all this?" the hostess, Barbara, asked me. "Isn't it just too beautiful? Where else in the world do you find such immediate physical beauty? Here in Paris it just makes me so happy to walk out on the street and breathe the air. I don't need anything else."

I was introduced to Roger, a famous French television producer. Jean-François, the publisher of the avant-garde magazine *The Underground Sun*, was there with his bubbly American girl-friend Judy. There was Ricardo Clementi, the Italian actor who had starred in some films by Jean-Luc Godard, and Patrick, a strikingly beautiful male model. I met William, the photographer born in Brooklyn who had made a name for himself doing tough street scenes shot from the hip and photos of models cast in stark and distant geographies. There was Titi, a Sengalese musician, who boasted that by standing on his head for an hour every morning he was able to remain in a state of a permanent "high." Finally, I met Charlie, an American painter born in Paris who knew Saul Bellow and James Jones and had come back to Paris on the GI Bill and stayed. From the theatrical world there was Maurice, the playwright *au succès*, with whom Ode had had a memorable, three-night affair. Meanwhile, Barbara made sure the food and champagne were served copiously, while she promoted and pushed her latest little book, *The Blue Stairs*.

"What happened to Pierre?" I asked Ode when I had a chance.

"Oh, Pierre? Ah, *oui*, well, he was not invited, because, *tu vois*, you see, he is too possessive, and he cannot stand for Cynthia to even see anyone else, so it was better for him not to come, or he would just have made a scene. You know, *tu sais*, we didn't even tell him we were having this party tonight. It's for Cynthia—and look at her, look how she shines, so beautiful and cool."

Right there I wanted to seize Cynthia and bring her to me and free her from the bizarre influence of the fiercely aloof and independent Ode. I was eager to know what would happen to us, how our fate would unfold. It's true that youth always seemed to have before it so many promises, but somehow I felt this was my last chance at love and life and I had to seize it—now.

Roger, the TV producer, was telling the party about a new project he hoped Cynthia would agree to. It would be a special documentary entitled "The Many Ways Women Say No."

Cynthia would be one of the women chosen to illustrate the "power of no." Roger wanted her filmed saying "no" in different voices and accents and intonations to a variety of men chosen at random. Her job would be to demonstrate to the French television audience how well she could say "no" just using her voice, her head, her gestures, her body.

Cynthia burst out laughing. "But how do you know so well that I am so good at saying 'no'?"

"I don't," Roger said. "Except that every time I tried to get you to have dinner with me, you always had something else to do."

"But suppose I did have a desire to say 'yes,'" Cynthia went on, her eyes sparkling, teasing.

"Then just say 'yes'!"

"Non, non, non!" she rapid-fire answered in French.

Everyone laughed. Champagne flowed, but the moment of gaiety did not last. Ode was explaining to Jean-François, the publisher of *The Underground Sun*, how she was seeking to free herself of her fear of death by washing corpses.

"Why not then make love to a corpse?" Jean-François asked. "It should be easy, *non*? The body's already stiff." He smirked.

"No, what would be really interesting would be to be present at the moment of their death, to be able to watch how they transit to the other side."

Cynthia nodded in agreement. She was just telling William, the American photographer known for his up-close street scenes in Harlem, about her latest dream.

"It was incredible, it lasted so long, like an eternity, and it was all about a magic stone—a large, cool, perfectly rounded, smooth stone. I felt such a deep connection between myself and this strange stone. Then out of nowhere words were whispered, and the last ones I remember were 'Go into the supremacy of stone.'"

"How about just getting stoned?" Jean-François snickered.

"I've got an idea," said William. "My publisher wants me to do a book that would be like a pilgrimage to historic places, like Stonehenge." He thought he could capture some "superb" photographs of Cynthia lying semi-nude and lizard-like on the old stones. He asked her, half-seriously, if she would be interested in traveling around the world with him, to do a "stone pilgrimage."

It was this conversation, I realized much later, that inspired Cynthia's wild trip later to the Acropolis in Greece and the pyramids in Egypt and eventually to the mountains in northern New Mexico and to the Arizona desert.

Cynthia smiled in that gentle, disarming way she had. "It was only a dream, guys. I don't do stones!"

"But how about getting stoned?" Jean-François insisted again.

A special brand of the highest quality Moroccan weed was produced, and Ode did the honors of rolling the joints. "This shit is called 'diamond-high,'" Ode explained. "It's so pure, it goes right to your head."

"Right," someone else said. "You know, if people smoked more grass, it would make them less violent."

"Can you get me another Black Label and soda?" Charlie asked Barbara. "I'm not into this drug thing. For me, it's wine or whiskey, preferably the latter."

Barbara brought him back his drink, measuring the miniscule ice cubes carefully.

"Why don't we do some hash?" Ricardo Clementi suggested.

"I was just reading about that," Barbara said. "You know, the word *hashish* comes originally from the Moroccan word *hasssasin*, which became our 'assassin.' They used those drugs to dull their minds so they'd be ready to kill."

I knew I didn't want to kill anyone; in fact, quite the opposite. And I knew I didn't want to depend on artificial stimulants to create a sense of happiness. So when the embossed water pipe was passed solemnly to me, as if in a religious ceremony. I declined. After a while, a cake was produced, and the evening sprang back to normal, with everyone singing "Happy Birthday, Dear Cynthia." They sang it in French and English, and Ode performed in Arabic. Barbara read one of her softly sensual poems from *The Blue Stairs*. The party found a second life and lasted till the early hours.

Cynthia seized my arms. Her eyes were moist with tears. I didn't know why. "It's just too much," she said, "too much, *de trop*."

"What's too much?"

"Everything tonight, being in Paris, this party, being here with you. Look," she changed the subject abruptly, "did you know Barbara spent last winter in

Marrakech? She rented a house. Come, let me show you the room she decorated here."

Cynthia led me away from the others into a small, pink room where a Moroccan lamp cast weird shadows on the walls, and colorful Moroccan cushions lay scattered over the floor. On the wall were black-and-white photos of the Atlas Mountains and the desert. Cynthia showed me a book that Barbara had made by hand that was filled with postcards, photos, images, and poems about the desert.

"This is my real dream," she said. "This is what Ode is teaching me. This simplicity. The beauty of these great, empty spaces. You know, she was born in the mountains in Morocco, but she actually grew up in the desert. She knows how to live there. That's what I want to learn to do, away from fashion and men and this goldfish bowl of Paris."

I was silent.

"Do you think you'd ever want to go live with me in the desert?" she asked me gently.

I was about to tell her that I didn't think I was ready to install myself in some version of the Sahara.

But before I could answer, she murmured, "You know, I just want to be alone with a man in the desert. Just him and me, standing and facing the wind, the sand, the stars. That's all."

"But why the desert?" I questioned angrily. "Why not some green island with water and light and trees, where we could relax and be alone together."

She put her fingers on my lips and mouthed wordlessly, *"Oui."*

But that night was not destined to be our first night together.

CHAPTER 16

▼

Alone in my Paris "hole in the ground" on rue Campagne-Irè, I wrote in my Paris notebook:

> *I wonder if I am capable of happiness. Do I have the equipment for it? The training? Is there a school for happiness I should have gone to? Or am I just too stupid to figure it out, to be able to answer the real question, actually the only question worth answering, which is how to live? And whether living well is even possible without being competent in matters of love and especially of sexual love. What I know is that I must continue this journey to the heart of love, the great, mysterious center.*

It kept getting more complicated, because Cynthia called and said, "Remember that American guy you met at Barbara's party the other night?"

"William, the photographer who wanted to take those pictures of you around the world?"

"No, I mean Charlie. You must remember Charlie, that bald-headed guy who's a painter."

"Yes, I remember him." What I remembered was the way he couldn't take his eyes off Cynthia—as well as all the scotch and sodas he consumed.

"Well, Charlie's great. I want you to get to know him. He's been in Paris longer than anyone—since the 1950s really. Did you ever hear of that artist who does the very thin sculptures, Alberto Giacometti? Well, Charlie was Giacometti's best friend. Charlie doesn't do sculptures, but I want you to see these incredible paintings he does, which are in the spirit of Giacometti."

"You mean, he's just copying something?"

"No, no, not at all. It's much more powerful than that. Charlie's obsessed with the female form. He has these models come and pose for him. He paints them nude sitting on chairs, over and over again. I feel very close to him in some way. I think you should know him."

Charlie and I finally met late one evening at Le Coupole on the boulevard Montparnasse, which looked like a dark river, channeled with cars, between the glowing lights of those famous other cafés, Le Select and Le Dome.

"Charlie's an old hand in Paris," Cynthia had told me. "He's taught me a lot. I think you should get to know him."

"Hello there, young man." Charlie introduced himself with a firm shake of the hand. He half-rose from the bench at Le Coupole. He was of medium height, bald, in his late fifties. He had an unusual head—hard and bullet-shaped—and dark, intent eyes. He was wearing a snap-front denim shirt and a rust-colored jacket with elbow patches. He reminded me of some old-time Chicago gangster.

"*Garçon!*" He snapped his fingers. He ordered another Black Label and soda with plenty of ice. The French were very sparing in their use of ice, as if it were some precious commodity.

"Hello there," Charlie went on. "Gee, how are you? I've heard so much about you from Cynthia. Me, I'm catching my breath. What a time."

"Why, what happened?"

"Oh, my god! At first the flies—countless flies in my studio. You've never seen so many of them in your life. Then I went to get my car to come and meet you and there's a damn garage strike going on. No one was there. I couldn't get my car, so finally I hailed a taxi and said, 'Le Coupole.' So I got in the cab but there was this big white van blocking the way in front of us, and the driver said we can't move, and I said something to him, and he swore back at me in some French slang I didn't understand, and just then these two men came out of the van and started unloading stretchers onto the sidewalk, and the driver honked his horn, and they said, 'Just a minute until we unload these bodies and then we'll get out of your way.' I guess there was a hospital there or something and they were delivering dead bodies from that night's rounds."

We talked for a while, and then Charlie asked me if I had eaten, and I said I hadn't. He hadn't either, so we ordered fresh white asparagus followed by an herb cheese omelette. Charlie kept sipping his Black Label and soda, and I had a half-bottle of cool Chablis. Charlie kept talking about Cynthia—how he had fallen for her at once, seduced by her freshness and liveliness and high spirits.

"How did you meet her?"

"It was right here at Le Coupole. She was with some people. I was sitting alone at the bar having a drink, and I just started noticing her because I look at things, you know. It all starts with the eyes, and the distance between things—the space—and she filled that space, and I was looking at her. Anyway, she came up to me afterwards and we just started talking, simply, like that, as if we'd known each other for a long time and were the best of friends."

"That's strange," I said, thinking of how I had met Cynthia in that psychiatric ward, listening at first to the notes of her silver flute as they floated by my iron-barred window.

"She's quick and she knows how to think and walk and brush her teeth," Charlie said, as if that summed her up. "I shouldn't have liked her so much, but I do. Damn! And you know, she's young enough to be my granddaughter."

Was this why Cynthia had so much wanted me to meet Charlie? Was it her own way of telling me that she already had another lover? I didn't know. What I did know was that she had a strange power she exerted on men that quickly drew them into her orbit. A mysterious tension established itself, born perhaps of a desire to know her and the simultaneous realization of how difficult a task that would be. It was not just because of her spontaneous, natural beauty. She herself was perhaps not even aware of it, and I wondered how long it would take me to figure out the secret that was drawing me to her.

Charlie ordered two espressos. He asked me if I would like to go with him to the Louvre early Sunday morning to look at the Egyptian room and the Fayoum portraits—those life-like portraits with the large, staring, immemorial eyes.

"Look," he said, smiling, "I just met you, but I can tell already that I like you. Paris is a tough place, and Cynthia is a tough girl. Maybe that's why she wanted us to get together, so we could share some stories and sympathize. But you know what I think? You're exactly the type of guy Cynthia needs. She doesn't need an old man like me. I'm just a kind of deluxe bum, a *clochard de luxe.* You're strong and young and smart and you've got a future. You can help Cynthia and she'll help you. She can show you and lead you onto a path you'd never be able to find by yourself. Can you understand that? So I'm out of the chase, man. I'm not going to pursue her any more. I think that's what she wanted. That's why she wanted you to meet me, that's what she wanted me to realize and say. So I'm saying it now, loud and clear to you: I give Cynthia to you, she's yours. Go now."

A few days later, I related this to Cynthia.

"Ha!" Cynthia laughed sharply. "You mean, Charlie thinks he can treat me like a trading card? It's not so easy!" She shrugged her shoulders as she rose and strode out through the revolving doors of Le Coupole.

It was the middle of August. Paris was virtually deserted. I followed her, caught up with her in front of the café Le Dome.

"Don't leave like that."

"But I'm mad at Charlie. Who does he think he is anyway, 'giving' me to you!"

"Look, it's obvious Charlie is attracted to you, but he's afraid of his feelings for you, so he just used me as an excuse to distance himself from you, that's all."

Cynthia considered this. Was it her own fault if she so easily inspired vital illusions in men?

"You don't understand," she said. "I could never be with Charlie. He's a great guy, but in his way of thinking, he's like a dinosaur. He goes to the Louvre every Sunday morning to look at those Egyptian and Etruscan things. Me, I want to create something different in my life, not just continue repeating the gestures of the past, can you get that?"

I looked at her, anxious to share in her dreams, but not exactly sure as to how I could participate.

"I want to change my focus," she continued. "Change my life. And why not? *Pourquoi pas?*" she asked rhetorically. "Life, perpetual change! That's what it is anyway. I've had enough of just one thing. I want all! *Je veux tout!*"

Cynthia seized me my hand, as if to indicate that, in some way, I would be included in this "everything."

I took her to Angelina's on rue de Rivoli where we tasted herbal teas and *patisseries*. Afterwards, as we went walking in the Tuileries gardens, Cynthia said that sometimes just breathing the French air and looking at the blue and silver cloud-torn sky gave her a sense of "limitless pleasure." We had dinner and went to see some "new wave" movie. Around midnight we got into a taxi, and I said, "Let's take a night-time tour of the Paris monuments."

"Okay," she said with enthusiasm, "but on condition that you let me see them upside down!"

She lay her much-loved head on my lap and I told the driver to drive, and he growled that he needed an exact destination, so I said how about the Arc de Triomphe and then the Pont Alexandre III bridge and the Eiffel Tower. The streaming red and green and white lights of Paris flashed by, Cynthia, still lying on my lap and looking up, while I softly caressed her hair. She seemed happy and delighted, her body quiet and radiant with an inner light. I began to get excited; she must have felt my sex stiffening, because she suddenly removed her head from my knees and sat up.

The lights of the ancient city of Paris gleamed magically and mysteriously as we rushed down the broad, tree-haunted boulevards. I wondered where this would lead us. All the ghosts in my heart were alive and urging me forward. I took her hand and she let me hold it.

Then she smiled wistfully, with a kind of contained emotion, and said, "I have to tell you something, I left Pierre. I've got another apartment. Would you like to see it? I'd love to show you my collection of stones."

She had them arranged in glass boxes. There were many smooth stones, some from the Normandy ocean shore, others from more exotic places she had visited on her photo shoots. There were some exquisite branches of coral. "I like bright things that are hard, that last," she said. "Because around me everything is always changing so fast."

She turned to me and touched my forehead with a gentle intensity. We were standing on the balcony of an apartment overlooking the phantasmagoric place Saint-Sulpice. "That church sometimes frightens me," she said. "Especially at night. It's so big and ghostly and grandiose."

"Yes," I said, hearing her voice as if it came to me from far away, a dream-like song.

"Do you see the lights on that far corner over there?" she continued. That's where the police station is—*les flics*. I know because when I first got to Paris I ran out of money—not even one *sou*—so I took a can of sardines from a supermarket and had to spend a few hours at that station over there. Finally they let me go."

I hugged her to me, wound the fragile ends of her blonde hair around my fingers.

"Cynthia," I said, "ever since I heard you playing the flute for me that night long ago in the psych hospital, I think I've been in love with you. Stay with me now. I need you."

Had she heard those words before? I felt her looking at me with a tender curiosity, as if I were an alien. Then she took me by the hand and led me inside. There were Moroccan rugs on the floor. Her silver flute lay on the table. There were a few black-and white photos of her in her modeling attire.

"Lie down," she said. "Close your eyes. Don't talk."

I obeyed. I wondered what was going to happen to her, to me, to us. It was hard for me to believe that finally she was ready to give herself to me.

She circled around me, drawing imaginary lines on the richly patterned carpets with her bare dancing feet.

It was easy to let myself be drawn into a trance-like state. I closed my eyes and saw multicolored explosions across the Paris sky. I saw sparks of blue and red light shooting out from the Eiffel Tower. I felt substantially happy, content with my fate. "No matter what happens," I repeated.

Then the pressure of her willowy body was against my chest. It stunned me to realize she had taken off her clothes. Lying nude fully extended on top of me, she breathed softly in my ear. She was whispering some mantra, perhaps designed to protect us from the consequences of what was about to happen.

I tried to reverse positions by turning her over, but she held fast. "Don't do anything," she told me. "Just lie there. Be peaceful. Feel free. Let life happen."

This is what I had dreamed of; it seemed inconceivable that the moment had finally arrived.

She was kissing my ears, my neck. She ran her tongue smoothly across my chest.

I felt my sex quickening, my muscles contracting into a hard mass that required liberation.

"What a big beast you are," she said. "You're a lion, a pure majestic animal. From now on your name will be lion, okay?"

I assented. I didn't know whether to purr or to roar.

She teased me again with her hands, letting her smooth pale skin flow against my own. I moved my hands down and grabbed her waist so I could control the movements of her calm curved haunches.

Surprisingly, neither resisting nor accepting, but passively, she let me thrust myself into her. As it happened, she gasped with a small cry of startled pain, then suddenly went limp, all the energy draining out of her body. She lay still above me, as if totally dependent on my strength to keep her alive, to keep her from falling.

I sensed in the flash of a second that my sex had become a weapon that, if I wished, I could use to manipulate her. That must have been what had frightened her. I thought, *Why has she so suddenly withdrawn into limp passivity?* But now I had lost control, plunging into her with a deep, relentless, driving passion. She whimpered and made small groaning noises but said nothing and did not plea for any mercy. She let me do whatever I wanted to her, my hands roving and exploring freely. She just relaxed and let it happen, as if overcome by the waves.

A doubt, a fear, came over me as the reality of the emotion crystallized. It was my turn to be consumed with wonder and fear over what was happening. So I sought to prolong the moment, to avoid any ending or talking about it afterwards. Finally I spasmed in an extended concussion that she accepted with limpid passivity. She smiled, started to say something, but did not, and was quiet.

"I don't know what will happen to us," she said finally. "I don't know if we can be together. But for now, for just this one moment more, let me enjoy this moment of being with you."

That moment would last three days. It was the limit she would allow, she said. If she was to keep her own sense of self and sanity, she needed to return to a certain solitude.

"But let's try to make it last longer," I argued. "Three nights is just not enough!"

"Remember what my friend Ode told you—it's a fact. It's the law of three nights. After that, everything goes downhill, and I don't want us to know that."

"Remember what the word *ode* means in German? It means emptiness, the desert, fucking nothingness!"

"That's okay," said Cynthia. "We are nothing, we come from nothing, we go to nothing."

"And you find that beautiful?"

"Yes, I do. But let's not talk about it, okay? We've got three days, let's live them as intensely as we can. Okay, my big lion?"

CHAPTER 17

▼

Cynthia and I stayed three days and three nights together. We did not talk about our past. We asked each other no questions. We made a conscious effort to live this relationship to the maximum, without commenting upon it, without trying to judge it or project it into the future.

"Let's just live it," Cynthia said. "Let's go as deep into it as we can, and not form any ideas about it—that can come later."

I took her to the heights of Montmartre and we stood on the terrace in front of that white wedding cake church, the Sacré Coeur. Below us, all of Paris with its terraced glistening slate roofs stretched out, and I felt for the first time that she truly belonged to me, that she and I and Paris were one, forming a kind of trinity.

I caressed her shoulders, her long, calm body. Cynthia seemed pleased. She smiled. She called me, *mon léon* (my lion). She hugged me and said that she, too, felt one with me.

Then she turned and looked out over the dark barrier at the bright ocean of the great city and said pensively, "You need to know that I can be with you but I cannot belong to you."

We walked back down the narrow, ancient stone steps. She was distant again. It was strange to be with Cynthia and at the same time to feel this longing for her, this weird and misplaced nostalgia, as if she represented something more than I could touch with my mere hands and flesh. And it was that extra "something" that gave me such a keen hunger and almost insatiable restlessness and desire.

"We are now, for the first time, going in the direction of history," she said

"And which is?" I wondered.

"Which is openness and communication and always going beyond boundaries. Paris is special because it's a place where exiles have always met and formulated their wild ideas. Paris has little to do with the French—it's the energy that artists, thinkers and doers have brought her. It's an energy center that radiates outward. You can feel that energy; it's what's passing through our bodies right now. Paris has a feminine energy. It's like when you arrive at the airport, the first thing you see is a sign that says '*Institut de Beauté.*' Paris is a chance meeting, it's *le hasard*, fate, destiny, the way things come together, that's all."

"It's what brought us together," I said. "Cynthia, I want to be with you."

"It's more like you just want sex," she laughed.

"Sex is not just about sex. It can also be used as a way of healing old wounds."

"What I want is to invent a new way of love that doesn't rely on jealousy and possessiveness and exclusivity."

"That sounds good, but I'm not sure if it's possible. Because then it wouldn't be true or authentic."

"Look," Cynthia said, grabbing my hand. "Let's not argue about what's true or real. Because what's real is I'm here. And I told you I'd be with you for three nights."

"That's absurd," I shouted. "This three-night rule is ridiculous!"

"We made a promise that we wouldn't talk about it. Before I came with you, remember, you said you would obey my conditions. Now be quiet."

She silenced me and pushed me back onto the bed. She took her flute and stood above me, her shadow flickering on the wall as she piped wild notes. She danced sinuously, her slender hips swaying and shimmering. I reached toward her but she slipped away, an elusive phantom.

"You only know desire like an animal knows it," she said reprovingly. "You respond to it with a blood rush.

"I'll show you a blood rush!" I said.

I seized her and drew her closer to me. She did not struggle when I lay her softly on the sheets. I hunkered down over her, pushing her smooth, much-loved thighs apart.

"Don't do it to me," she murmured. "I can't love you like this—I'm so afraid."

I felt I had no choice but to insist, to try to conquer her fear. So I pushed hard into her. She groaned, and in a kind of panic started tearing at my hair. But I continued. She submitted.

Strangely passive, her long sphinx-like body lay on my bed in the dark corner of my subterranean dwelling. After a while she sighed and said quietly, "You know, this 'man-woman' thing, I really don't understand much about it."

On the third day Cynthia said solemnly, "Tomorrow I will leave you. If you care for me at all, do not call me or come after me or try to find me. Let me go. I'll be here in Paris, and you will be here in Paris, and we will think about each other very much, but we cannot be together. Not now."

I took her to an "in" bistro for dinner on the quai Voltaire, then afterwards to the Closerie des Lilas for a nightcap. She sat quietly and looked at me with her large, grave eyes and sipped a *citron pressé*. I had a sense that I was losing her and drank more than I should have. We walked back to my underground studio and made love slowly and softly and sadly. I felt her spirit was already gone, and the next morning when I awoke, the hollow space next to me on the bed where she had slept was full of her absence.

CHAPTER 18

▼

Letters can bring hope or signal violent changes in direction, or even death. I had met Cynthia in the elevator when I was going to get my mail at American Express. Now I received, slipped under my door, an official-looking letter telling me that I had been drafted for the Vietnam War and was to report for military service.

I was instructed to show up at the American Hospital in Neuilly for a physical. My life in Paris, which for me was just beginning, now threatened to come to a sudden and unexpected end. There would be no more talk of painting or art or literature. My quest for life, the search for love, the mystery of Cynthia—all would have to wait. What I had found, I was about to lose. I didn't believe in the war and didn't want to be sent to fight in a war I did not believe in. I was nervous and afraid and not sure of what to do. But there was no choice.

So, on a gloomy dark winter morning, with the Paris sky hanging like a leaden cover over the city, I took the metro to the Neuilly station and walked the few blocks to the American Hospital, wondering if I would find Ode there, at work washing and purifying the bodies of dead people. I felt I was about to become dead myself.

I was interviewed by a Dr. Arnon, a short fidgety Frenchman with a moustache. He seemed ill at ease having to question an American about his psychological suitability for the Vietnam War. My internment at that psychiatric ward in New York City had showed up on my record, and now they wanted to see if I was mentally fit to go to Vietnam.

The interview was over quickly. Dr. Arnon asked me if I knew what a conscientious objector was.

I said I did, but I hadn't come to Paris for that reason. I had come to Paris to put a distance, or an ocean, between myself and my problems with growing up in America, and yet I still couldn't totally make a break, as the Vietnam War had crept up on me and was threatening to change my own life, as well as to take me away from Cynthia. I could not help wondering whether my fear of the war, and of being engaged in it, in some way reflected my fear of being vulnerable with Cynthia. I didn't know. These were things I had to find out.

Dr. Arnon asked me if I was aware that the French had had a long and bitter experience in Vietnam.

I said, yes, I knew.

He then asked me in a cool, neutral tone if I was in favor of the Vietnam War.

I told him that I most definitely was not in favor.

Then he looked intently at me as if deciding what my fate was going to be. After what seemed like a long time he said, "Okay, young man, I want you to tell me in your own words why you don't want to go to Vietnam?"

"It's very simple," I said. "It's because I don't believe in killing people."

He nodded, a faint smile coming over his tight features. "I'm going to give you a 4F rating," he said. "I'm going to declare that you're mentally unfit to serve in the Vietnam War."

My heart jumped up a mile inside me and I felt like reaching out over the well-worn metal table where Dr. Arnon sat and hugging him. I knew I could not be both authentic to myself and patriotic in the classic sense of the word. If coming to Paris was to find a sense of spirituality, of some meaning, how ironic it would have been if the end result had been my being drafted into the Vietnam War. But now that wasn't going to happen.

And so I returned joyfully to Paris, *la ville-lumière*, a free man.

CHAPTER 19

▼

I lingered in Paris. I knew I should return to the States, that I had no justifiable reason for staying, but somehow I could not tear myself away. I was searching for a chimera, a vision, a dream of sensual fulfillment and beauty. Far from assuaging my hunger, the fact that I had lived through a cycle of three days and three nights with Cynthia only worked to increase it. I desperately wanted her back again. One more time—even just one more night and day with her—was my obsession and relentless desire. It was hard to explain, but I felt that I both knew her and did not know her at the same time. It suddenly became clear to me that what I needed and desired was the space of the fourth night.

Late in the evening I would go restlessly walking down the long, vaulted, ghost-filled arcades of rue de Rivoli. In the distance beckoned the glittering lights of the place de la Concorde. Even the billboards gleamed in a special way, and the street kiosks shone wet in the rain. I would go up to one and buy the latest *Herald-Tribune*, thinking of the days not so long ago when I was selling that newspaper on the Champs-Elysées; and I would search for images of Cynthia flipping through the pages of the fashion magazine *Paris Style*.

Everything in Paris was special: the washed-out gray houses with their tall windows, the cropped treetops, the angled roofs with their chimney pots. Every dark, narrow street was an invitation to an infinite number of meetings and possibilities. It was life, at last, and I was living it. It was the center, and I was no longer just moving toward it—I was in it, caught up and circulating within the hermetic secrets of the grand, old, circular woman-city.

Without warning, Cynthia reappeared one afternoon. Flashing a bright smile as if nothing had happened, she rushed in with some colorful blow bubbles. It was a tarnished, slate-gray, cool Paris day. Cynthia came up to me and hugged me in silence for a long time. Then she blew some of the iridescent bubbles over the bed. The bubbles floated in front of the Egyptian posters I had hung, which showed images of camels, palm trees, and pyramids. Tossing off her shoes, she jumped on the mattress and started singing, "I'm a bubble, I'm a bubble born from a bigger bubble, a greater bubble, and giving birth to many bright, new, shiny bubbles. Here, a bubble for you, a beautiful bubble for us ..."

She was strange and crazy and sweet, captivating but unseizable.

I joined in her game, spouting, "No, you're not a bubble, you're a breath, you explode and disappear, you come and go, you're here and not here, you're not so much a woman as a fantasy, a glimpse of a dream, a floating sensation ..."

She turned suddenly to face me. She trapped my head between her hands and shook it hard, as if to wake me up. "Don't you know," she questioned. "But don't you know!" It was not so much a question as a harsh statement of fact.

"I feel too old and tired to know," I muttered. "Maybe once I knew. Not any more."

I had known once, I thought, when I was a kid lying on my back on the grass in the farm fields outside of Buffalo, staring up at the enormous night sky, and wondering about all the marvelous things that I felt deeply in my heart were surely going to happen.

Cynthia was fascinated by weapons, knives, images of sudden destruction. She loved that part in Dostoyevsky where he is brought to stand in front of a firing squad but it is a fake execution. Once, when I asked her how she wanted to live her life, she had answered with one word, "*Vite.*" Quickly. *La vie vite.* Life quickly.

Although we shared living space together, I did not succeed in possessing her. She would still disappear for days at a time. She herself did not know where she was going, nor could she say when she would be back. There was never any way to contact her. Even Ode did not know.

It was true I was painfully jealous of her absences, but she had forewarned me: "The one condition I have is that you impose no conditions. If you love me, you must love my freedom. If you cannot accept my freedom, then you cannot love me."

The elusive, memorably exotic, bright-spirited, impulsive, unseizable, eternally ephemeral woman-girl ...

In this way, without repeating themselves or leaving a trace, the months went by in Paris and evolved into years.

When Cynthia was with me, she would express her energy by bounding up on the wooden benches and round stone pedestals that lined the edges of sidewalks and driveways. Any object was a pretext for her to jump on it so that she could skip and dance. Her inner energy would run for a long time at a high level and then abruptly collapse. At night, exhausted, she would sleep like a rag doll, her arms dangling limply over the side of the bed, her head almost falling off the mattress, her body slanted. But if I tried to touch her sleeping form, she would wake up instantly, as if by an electric shock. I joked and said, "Cynthia, you don't so much sleep as hover on top of a sleeping state, from which you can wake up at any time with instant awareness."

"I sleep only to dream," she answered. "The purpose of my life is to live out the dream."

Cynthia's dreams were deep, crystalline, intense, fragmented with strange sexual images.

"All the time that I was dancing," she recounted a typical dream, "I thought that I would return to the chateau. O the chateau! The chateau! My life here was all false, all a mystery, there was nothing coherent or logical about it. But, every time I danced, I thought that I could get nearer to the chateau, that somehow, magically, I could approach it."

On another night, instead or the chateau or the castle, it would be: "I remember I was whirling and spinning like one of those Turkish dervishes. Suddenly a strange man who was holding a sort of perfume vial in his hand walked up and sprayed me all over with it. Immediately afterwards, I lost all my powers. I was forced to submit myself to this man. He tortured me by trying to find a name that would fit me. I kept insisting that I had no real name, but he would not listen. Finally, I bowed my head and wept because I didn't want to have a name. This man told me I would have to learn how to speak Latin because he was going to give me a Latin name, Felicita, and I would never be able to speak again unless I learned that ancient language."

Ode interpreted her dream this way: "When Cynthia finds the roots of her true self, only then will her whole being be transformed into 'happiness.'"

It was hard for me to understand why I longed for her in the way that I did. It drove me crazy, and there was nothing I could do about it. While Cynthia slept, I would sit beside her, watching over her like a sentinel, not venturing to touch her, not wishing to wake her out of her profound dream state. I would spend hours hunched over her, imprinting on my brain every curve of her body and scent of her pale skin and blonde hair. It was as if I had become the night watchman, the vigilant guardian of her unconscious state.

As I observed her during those long hours, I wanted to say to her, "Cynthia, Cynthia, in your simplicity, your child-likeness, you're amazing passion for life, what will become of you? Where will a spirit such as your own end up?"

Later, on distant August evenings, strolling down the leafy tree-canopied sidewalks of the boulevard Edgar Quinet, I would stop and press her smooth body against the stony walls of the Montparnasse cemetery. She lay on top of the black marble of Brancusi's tomb and I kissed her under the graveyard stars.

When I questioned her about the future, she always responded in the same sibylline way, "Don't wonder, don't worry," she would urge softly. "When the moment is ready, it will happen."

Exactly what was going to happen, she didn't say, and I didn't know. I had to content myself with her presence, and the boundless yearning she made me feel.

Yet the old nagging question of why I was in Paris and how long I should stay returned. An old friend from St. Paul's wrote me, "You always wanted to live in an artificial paradise. I know that's why you're staying in Paris and exactly why you should leave tomorrow morning." But was it so wrong to believe in the promises I had once made to myself? The reason for being in Paris was simple: to live a peak moment or die. If life was worth living, it had to be underlined with passion, sex, love—all fused into the exuberant truth of one feeling. And I was intent on seizing that moment as it actually took place, just as it was cresting, so to speak, on the edge of the breaking moment-wave.

Still, during the long, dark, damp days of the winter months, with the soiled gray sky hanging low over the city like a coffin lid, and with Cynthia often absent on her modeling shoots, it was not easy to maintain a sense of harmony and balance. One day the concierge found me crying crumpled up on the floor, knees to my chest. I had stopped locking the door. My feeling was: if people want to come in, let them. There was nothing to hide or protect any more.

One afternoon Cynthia arrived unexpectedly. As usual, she embraced me without saying anything. Then, kissing the back of both my hands gently, she said, "You look terrible. Don't be sad. Don't be afraid."

"I can't stand it any more," I confessed. "Paris is not what I thought it would be."

"Nothing is ever like we think it will be."

"But I want to get out," I said. "Jump out if necessary. I've simply had enough. *Assez.*"

"You can't jump out of what is," she advised sagely. "And I thought you loved Paris and you wanted to be here."

"Things in Paris are too old. It's a fossilized city, living on the phantoms of the past. And it makes me feel too alone. As if the people around me are slowly dying. And I don't want to die here."

"What do you want then?"

"I want to go the desert or the mountains with you and be alone in a cool, empty space with nothing but you and me to face the emptiness we know is all around us."

"It would be wrong for you to go, and I couldn't do that with you. You're just trying to forget."

"Forget what?"

"The oppressive character of your own self. *You* are only doing this to *you*. No one else is. You do it to yourself. You must like it or you wouldn't be doing it."

"But it's not just me. It's my self. My stubborn body with its mixed salad of desires. This whole fucked-up society."

"I'm sorry you feel so blocked."

"Yes, even suffocated by all these things I don't understand. And then there is you …"

"I am not a magic word," Cynthia reminded me. "So tell me what you want."

"I want you, Cynthia. I want to live more with you. I need to feel that you belong to me, that we are together here."

"But that's so wrong," she said advisedly. "The more you live with me, the more you'll find that I don't belong to you, that I don't belong to anyone. You'll only be sadder if I give myself to you as completely as you want. Can't you understand that? You are not ready."

Cynthia repeated these words many times, with ever-shifting variations, but always arriving at the same irrevocable conclusion: I was not ready. But what was the secret test or initiation I had to pass? How could I let go enough so that Cynthia would think I had let go completely?

For some time I did not see Cynthia. She was traveling to do her photo shoot jobs. I found myself again alone in Paris. Happiness was my shadow—I saw it and chased it but somehow could not incorporate it into my being.

I received some postcards from Cynthia postmarked Tunisia. On the back of one she had written, "Life is haunted, like a house. You are my ghost. I shall return."

But more and more what interested me was the path to freedom. Freedom, in my case, meant deliverance from the past and its stealth phantoms of sexual desire and romantic love. Tirelessly, like a mantra, I repeated: You have to live now. What counts is the *now*. Be a *now man*. So *now*, get up and move, one foot after the other—go!

I sought my identity in other places.

I moved into an anonymous apartment building on the outskirts of Paris. Rows and rows of windows created simulacrums of identity. I became a door at the end of a corridor, a number among hundreds. I wanted to be invisible, to walk through a disappearing machine and never return.

My third-world neighbors woke me up with their screaming. I heard a woman shouting, "I can't take it! I just can't take it! *Non! Non!*"

From my window I saw her rush out onto the street. A passing taxi nearly hit her. I saw her fall down screaming, soon surrounded by passersby and *gendarmes* (cops).

I spent days without going out, without talking to anyone. I read Proust's *Remembrance of Things Past*—all seven volumes, in the original French

The concierge and his wife, a couple from Barcelona, told me they were passionately interested in crime. Every time I passed by their *loge*, one of them would come out and happily tell me how many people had been murdered in Paris the day before and under what circumstances.

I closed the windows and wore earplugs to create a wall of silence around me. I wanted it that way; I thought, *If I can blanket out all sound, all noise and distraction, perhaps I can attune myself to purer, deeper vibrations.*

I saw things getting smaller—the table, the windows, the walls. Everything shrunk. I thought, *Soon there will be nothing at all. I will have created a desert in the midst of thousands of people in this poor, horribly noisy suburb.*

Finally I received another postcard from Cynthia. On the front were jungle animals that were barely recognizable as she had drawn funny comments and sketches on each one of their faces. On the back she had written, "Let me know when you are finally free."

What did she mean? I wondered. What was "finally free"?

She had added a post script: she was coming back to Paris.

Cynthia arrived at Orly Airport, returning from Tunis. She seemed happy, almost joyous, to see me. She spun around in the sonorous airport hallway, cavorting, laughing, tossing her head, squeezing both my arms.

"I've decided I want to be with you!" she declared. "All this time away from you has cleared my head up. Let's try! Oh please, *s'il te plait*, let's try, *essayons*, okay?"

I pulled her luggage off the baggage carrousel. I wondered if she meant what she said, and if what she said was real.

"Why don't we get married?" she threw out suddenly.

Amazed, I started to answer, "Do you think—?"

"Yes, it just feels right, no?"

As the cab took us back to the Porte d'Orléans, I wasn't sure exactly what I felt. I had been so close to her at times, and at other times so terribly distant, that it was hard to know, in this relationship, what was true and what was illusion. But I wanted so much to believe it, I held her and pulled her to me and kissed her on the mouth.

Later she tried to explain her return and sudden change of heart. "No more yesterdays," she said. "You have no idea how everything from the past came back and hit me when were doing photos at that oasis in Tunisia."

She paused, pushed her hair back with one hand, and continued, "I'm so sick of thinking about yesterday, and then the day before yesterday, and all the terrible yesterdays that keep us from going forward. You know what they say—today is the first day of the rest of your life. That's how I want it be, now, from this very moment forward."

Of course, I agreed. I knew that we had to keep going forward, to sustain that essential illusion of progress.

"If we're going to be together," she said, "let's try to make sure that every day is different, however slightly, from the one before."

And so it was. We sought to attune ourselves to the most subtle shades of vibration and aura, learning to distinguish among them, to find which had the most beautiful radiance.

Because we were talking about marriage, I took Cynthia to a service at the Russian Orthodox Church on rue Daru. It was a rich, mysterious ceremony, the deep voices of the Russian priests swelling up in grave intonations behind the gilded, icon-laden partitions. There we met the famous American Zen spokesman from Sausalito, California, Allan Watts. He was much taken by Cynthia— her spark, her spontaneity. He took me aside and said, "She's such a free spirit, she has almost no baggage."

"What do you mean?" I asked.

"I mean, man, if you want to be with her, just learn to carry your own bags, they're heavy enough and it'll take you some time to get used to them."

More and more, I had the clear impression that I had outdistanced many things. I felt like a runner who has gone beyond the pack and is now essentially confronting himself, his own stamina and endurance.

But, as Allan Watts reminded me, "There are many levels, and you may have just reached the first one."

CHAPTER 20

▼

Spring came again and Cynthia was with me and we were happy. To celebrate the spirit of being together, we took the overnight train from the gare de Lyon and traveled south to Spain, to a Mediterranean beach and the ocean. We explored the beaches around Barcelona. We were having a café and a Coca-Cola in a small fishing village when a distinguished-looking, older man in a crisp, white linen suit approached us and asked us if we would like to join him for a drink on his yacht. His name was Gaston, he said, and we later learned his last name was Morgan, like the bank. He didn't have to work, he said, and traveled around the world on his yacht. He couldn't help noticing Cynthia, and it was easy to see that he was totally captivated by her.

That night we set sail with Gaston Morgan on his yacht to the tiny primitive island of Formentera.

"I feel so relaxed," Cynthia said. "We can do anything we want. Life's an adventure, let's just live it."

Formentera was a remote island—in those days not so popular—where most of the stone houses had no running water or electricity. We stayed in the top of a restored windmill. Gaston was a charming host and entertained us by candlelight in the evening with his many international stories. During the day we explored the small island. Cynthia found an isolated cliff jutting out over the blue waters and there, on a huge stone, she lay bare-chested, exposed like a sacrifice to the sun. "This is a time of no time," she said. "This is a place of no place. Let's not talk. Words will only hurt us. Let's just feel and be."

It was obvious she was going further and further into her own trip—not so much toward nature as toward a new and spontaneous naturalness, where she could be naked and one with water, sky, and stone, not feeling any substantial difference between herself and the material world, even her flesh becoming the same as the warm, worn stone or the blue, waving water.

I touched her; she let me touch her. She did not move. She knew that I was touching her but she said nothing. There was just the feeling between us of her letting me touch her. It felt good. Her body was light and fine, and it was hard just to touch her and to keep from moving beyond the touching to the actual possessing.

We would fall asleep later on a large mattress on the upper floor of the stone windmill, the clear luminous light of the stars piercing in through the massive carved out windows.

Early the next morning, with the sun rising, we went walking along the steep Formentera cliffs. Cynthia climbed nimbly over the rocks, looking for shallow rock pools. She moved up and down along the path that wound around the age-old stones, her body like a ribbon of light that flickered and sent signals to me.

We came to a protected small, pristine cove, and she took her clothes off and flung herself into the waves and swam out as far as she could until I was worried because her head had become a faint smudge on the horizon.

I heard Gaston calling us, as the wind was rising and he wanted us to get back to his yacht.

Cynthia swam back, her hands caressing the waves, the waves rippling in over the sand-packed stones. What was she looking for? I wondered. Silence? Grace? Ease?

"Above all," she said, "great ease with everything and with myself."

Later she lay down on the back of the yacht. She slept. Gaston was in his cabin downstairs. I sat next to her and touched her shoulder and she did not move. Delicately I stroked and then gently sucked at her bare breasts. She let me suckle them. She murmured that she was very tired from wandering over the cliffs; she did not want to have any sex right now. She said we could have sex later, there would be much time later for sex. I should not hurry or be anxious now.

Her pale, smooth body absorbed the haze-dazzled afternoon Mediterranean light. Cynthia seemed an ineradicable part of the scene, born into it. I loved her then for her strength and fragility. I felt in my heart that she was mine without being mine because she could never be anyone else's.

It had been a quick wonderful trip to Formentera. So much had been accomplished and nothing had truly been said. Gaston invited us to stay on his yacht, to continue traveling with him. We took a taxi from the port to the train station, stopping to wonder in the afternoon shadows at the extravagantly tortured forms of the Gaudi cathedral. Cynthia said Spain was too religious and cruel and she couldn't wait to cross the frontier back into *la douce France*.

CHAPTER 21

▼

Once again we were in Paris. I bought the *Herald-Tribune* and, over a *grand-crème* and freshly baked almond croissants, found that Americans had just completed the first manned docking of two space stations. The idea of sending rockets to the moon made Cynthia laugh.

The French newspapers were quick to declaim, "The Americanization of outer space."

"What about inner space?" Cynthia wondered.

There was always the vital question that hung between us of whether we should return to America.

"I'll never go back to the States," Cynthia vowed. "So much of what's happening there isn't really necessary."

"What do you mean?"

"I mean it's the continuous production of things for which no genuine need is felt. That need must be artificially stimulated and aroused. In the US of A, to be "with it" you must buy. If you can't buy, you're doomed, out of it, you don't exist. Those who are "out" today are the young, the poor, and the black."

I didn't know why she was being so cynical. But even Paris suddenly depressed her. "There are too many people here!" she declared. "Paris would be great if there weren't so many French people! They're too sarcastic and domineering. I can't take myself seriously here. And all the men do is talk about sex and wanting to sleep with me, that's all that's on their minds, so I spend most of my time devising strategies to elude their constant advances."

I still was in love with her and desired her more than ever. She said she loved me, but she still acted evasively, from time to time showing the need to demonstrate her independence.

She came into a café with an African-American wearing blue work dungarees with suspenders. "This is Ted. He's a jazz poet and my new friend. He also does practical things, like build beds. And ..." she whispered to me, "he looks like a good lover."

"I can't believe it!" I said to her angrily. "I mean, you're even thinking about sleeping with that beat poet, Ted?"

"Who said I was?" she defended herself. "He's just a friend, a really good poet, a friend of André Breton and all the surrealists."

"Listen," I warned her, "before you go getting your feet wet again, perhaps it's important to know how you'll get them wet and what will happen after they're wet."

She laughed in her bright, vivacious way. "But I want to go hip hop and up! And leap forward and jump into life!"

I didn't see her again for three or four days. I didn't know if she was with Ted or not. It was again almost the end of summer. When Cynthia was absent, I would set a simple goal of forcing myself to take long random walks every night with one condition: that I would desire nothing. My operating instructions were: don't torment yourself thinking of what might be. Instead, focus your mind on what you are living, get inside your own life, inhabit it, know it. Whatever you need is there, in that circle of consciousness, no need to go outside. I joked about myself as a college drop-out/black sheep/rebel much too taken up with a beautiful but unstable young woman who wouldn't give herself to him, at least in the conclusive, definitive way he longed for. Therefore, in cleansing solitude, I prepared to strip away from my life everything that was non-essential.

CHAPTER 22

▼

Suddenly, miraculously, I was with her again. She came late one night and again scratched at my window from outside, just like a cat. "Come with me," she urged. "We have to go now."

I hailed a cab and we rushed through red and green streaming lights along the boulevard to the train station, the Gare de Nord—another departure.

Gloria Stein, her designer friend, had offered Cynthia the use of her flat in London. We could stay there until Friday. Cynthia was happy. She told Gloria, "I just want to live and be happy and not be weighed down by things. I'd like to live in a tent. A tent would solve all my problems!"

Gloria was a small, round-fingered, overweight, middle-aged expatriate from Chicago, whose body looked as if it had been gutted by sweets. She said she dreamt of ice cream parlors, of sitting in a bar that served only ice cream cones in fabulous colors and flavors.

Gloria had sent Cynthia a postcard that showed an American space station circling the earth. On the back she had written, "I need to know you better. We are still too far apart."

Cynthia told Gloria her dream: a white globe appeared. Children approached it. Some stood, some sat; they ventured to touch it; they moved slowly around it. Approaching the ball—the globe—became a religious act. That act was performed with slowness and ceremony and precision."

I interpreted the dream to mean that Cynthia would not allow herself to become involved with Gloria because their relationship would never be whole and complete.

Gloria expected love but had no idea how to find it. The possibility of love made her exuberant. She was not capable of doing anything practical or functional, but she thought she was capable of love. She had ample hips and imposing thighs that jutted forward in a challenging way. It was her openness, her surprising, almost savage, frankness that attracted Cynthia.

Cynthia said, "Gloria needs love but is not able to love. No man will ever fulfill her."

I felt the relationship with Gloria brought Cynthia closer than ever to renouncing and rejecting the feminine side of her own sexuality. Sensing a new problem, desperately I would try to talk Cynthia out of her blossoming relationship with Gloria. But when we returned to Paris, Gloria came with us.

One night at Le Coupole, Cynthia said, "I always smile and try to look happy and everyone thinks I'm happy, but I never really succeed. I know it's a mask. I'm a failure at my own happiness."

"The problem is," Gloria answered, "that you're trying to prove something. Of course, there's nothing ever to prove or to feel guilty about. Stop trying to do something for the sake of your parents whom you probably will never see again, and stop trying to measure yourself in terms of what men think they want."

Had Cynthia slept with Ted, the beat poet and bed builder? I wasn't sure, especially since meeting Gloria, the sexual object—for Cynthia—had become impossible. She had become afraid of the penis. She said she could never get used to the idea of "that thing" being forced inside her. She now thought sex was a mistake, an aberration. Gloria fully encouraged her in this demented way of thinking.

I had no choice but to grit my teeth and think, *What can I possibly do to change this? And why bother? What difference does it make?* But I was lying to myself—it made all the difference in the world, because I was in love with her. I loved her for her elusiveness and fragility and strangeness and even basic incompatibility with me or anything that could possibly resemble a normal life.

Gloria's physique kept her from being marked out as a sexual victim. She struggled toward a new orientation, relying on the gift of her generous emotions. Cynthia dined with her often on the terrace of her apartment. They gave each other firmness and strength. They spoke without ever raising their voices in a kind of low-keyed conspiratorial whisper. Cynthia often used the words "firmness and strength" in describing what Gloria gave to her. I would grow impatient and interrupt, "The weekend is coming. Can't we do something alone, by ourselves?"

"We've got to do something!" she mimicked.

"There must be some good parties or feasts we can go to."

"I'm thinking about what I'm going to do if you—"

"You're always thinking about what you're going to do ..."

"But, really, what about this weekend? We don't have to stay in Paris. There are so many places we could be. Just think, we could be in India, or Peru ..."

Cynthia spent that weekend with Gloria. Gloria served as a refuge for her, a quiet haven of ordinariness. Gloria had already fumbled her life. Never married, it was as if she'd been born to boredom and unfulfilled expectancy. She was always waiting for something that could never possibly happen. She had lived in London and San Francisco and Ibiza and Taos. She said she now wanted to go to Fez and then to an ashram in Malakara in the most southern part of India. She told everyone who would listen to her that her desire was no longer for love but for harmony with herself and peacefulness. But somewhere, I thought, she also had hatred or anger, or self-pity turned into anger or hatred, because she would say things like, "What I rage against is all the bullshit of America!"

Cynthia and Gloria discussed their projects for departure. They were endlessly plotting some form of imaginary escape that would conceivably bind them together for always.

"There's no need for us to stay in Paris."

"We could be anywhere at all. We could be in Africa in the 'Village of Lions.'"

Gloria: "Isn't it amazing to think of all the airplanes that are constantly coming and going? What temptations! What possibilities!"

"Let's make sure we leave soon."

"All we have to have to do is have our passports, a toothbrush, and a few francs ..."

On a Sunday, Cynthia, Gloria, and I went for a picnic to the forests outside of Paris. A bearded Frenchman was chasing a woman. He almost stumbled over us. Cynthia called out. Other picnickers looked up, startled. The pursued young woman ran in and out between the tall trees like a white rabbit. The man kept chasing her. Cynthia and Gloria sat and watched, their hands loosely linked together. It made me wonder again what I was doing there. What had led me to accept this absurd situation?

Gloria hugged Cynthia. They seemed closer together than ever. But Gloria insisted that I hug both of them and in this way we would celebrate a sense of communality.

But I liked Gloria because she could be kind and soft and generous, as well as being Cynthia's good friend. One of Gloria's favorite expressions was, "What a lot of crap." I liked this non-pretentious simple side of her. What I disliked was the hold she had on Cynthia.

Gloria told me that, when one of her boyfriends came to see her in the morning, he had the habit of greeting her with, "Bonjour, Bullshit."

It was cruel, Gloria agreed, but perhaps it was true, because she said she had lived so much bullshit in America that part of it must be permanently residing in her, even in Paris. After many years in so many foreign places, she thought she was contaminated with "bacterial bullshit."

Cynthia and Gloria would encourage each other with the idea that, while it was sad to be against so much civilization, if one wanted to be true and honest with one's self, one had to move in a different direction, against science and technology and the military and psychoanalysis and the government and capitalism and—Fortunately, after two weeks of this, Cynthia had had enough, and I was happy when Gloria finally took the Golden Arrow overnight train and ferry back to her apartment in London.

CHAPTER 23

▼

That autumn it rained softly in Paris and we stayed most of the time indoors. Cynthia bought some goldfish, naming the prettiest one Souki. We would lie on the floor on the Moroccan cushions and carpets and listen to new music like the Beatles or early Bob Dylan. When Cynthia wasn't modeling, she would spend endless hours at her sewing machine making fantasy clothes, often in an oriental style. Or she would play her silver flute while I reclined and read Aldous Huxley's *The Doors of Perception*. There was an elaborately carved water pipe that we used to inhale the finest quality hashish, invariably supplied by Ode or her friends. "It puts your mind in a state of euphoria," Cynthia said. "It's like orgasm, except longer and better."

On Monday mornings, the Spanish concierge never failed to tell us in proud tones how many French citizens had died in traffic accidents on the highways that weekend.

One night, when we came out of the underground station at Étoile, a strange man, dressed in black, complete with a top hat and a cane, nodded to Cynthia and tapped his cane three times. "What's that?" I wondered. "A secret signal?"

In the warm fog, a blue Peugeot was chasing a black Citroen down the never-ending Champs-Elysées. When we got back to the apartment, there was a letter under the door from Gloria in London, who wrote, "If we cannot attack American politically through outer experience, then perhaps we can attack it sexually, through inner experience."

I had met Judy, a blue-eyed, perky American girl, at Barbara's birthday party for Cynthia at her duplex on the quai des Grands-Augustins. Judy's boyfriend, Jean-François, used some of the money he inherited from his family (significant shareholders in Total Petroleum S.A.) to publish one of the first French anti-establishment magazines, *The Underground Sun*. He had written a number of left-wing articles severely critical of the American involvement in Vietnam. I told him how grateful I was that, thanks to the sympathies of a French doctor, I had not been drafted. Judy loved French lingerie. She showed Cynthia how she had collected boxes and boxes filled with underwear—bras and panties. "I really have a hard time throwing anything out," she said. "I guess I just like the feeling of being drawn down and sucked into my possessions."

"What does Jean-François think?"

"He tells me I should get rid of all the stuff."

Cynthia decided to help Judy put some order in her flat and clean everything out. I helped her carry crates overflowing with underwear and woman's clothing down six flights of stairs.

"Don't all these bundles of clothing we're carrying out look just like corpses?" Cynthia remarked. "You cast them off but the spirit remains."

The protests against the Vietnam War were increasing; at some universities students had set fire to cars. In other cities, there were reports of workers rioting and taking control of the streets. Ted, Cynthia's beat poet pal, declared, "Look, man, socialism, which is the desire for equality, will ultimately triumph over capitalism, which is always for the benefit of the successful few."

"Hahaha!" I could hear Cynthia laughing, her laughter streaming down the gray zinc light of the studio into the bathroom, where she stood nude in the shower, singing, "America the great, America the beautiful, my country you are part of me …"

Later as I lay on top of her, she said she wasn't going to move, she wanted to try to be completely still. She asked me if I could make love to her without rippling her pale smooth surfaces. But when I came inside her with a violent thrust, she shook me by the shoulders and told me to stop, that it should not begin that way. She asked me to withdraw, to go slowly and tenderly, and then begin again. I loved her and listened to her and did what she wanted me to do.

I fell asleep, dreaming of a long, black light in the shape of a spear that came crashing through the side of my head. I was lying on the studio floor on a thick, hard mattress with no sheets and a crumpled colorful Moroccan blanket that Cynthia had brought back from an *Elle* magazine job in Marrakesh. Through the tall windows that gave onto the cobbled alleyway, a rough sea of passersby could be heard. The morning light rubbed along the low, pink walls. I tried to situate myself, to establish an identity in this strange new space we had just moved into. I was not sure whether the Cynthia lying beside me was real or not. I had already found and lost her many times. Her various images flashed in sharp spots through my mind. She was telling me about a trip she had taken some time ago.

"It was with that painter, Charlie, remember him? He had this big Buick and he took me driving along the steep cliffs in Normandy, where the Germans once had their machine gun nests. The coast was rocky and austere. It began to rain. Charlie surprised me by embracing me suddenly and saying he loved me. He said, 'I booked a room at the Hotel Normandy, let's go back there and have a drink.' I said no, I just wanted to stay on the beach and walk. He said, 'Even in the rain?' I said, 'Yes, even in the rain.' But it got cold and dark and we did go back to the hotel and sat in the lobby in front of a fireplace, and Charlie got me drinking Johnny Walker. It made me sick, and I left in the early morning and took the train back to Paris. I didn't see Charlie again until that party at Barbara's."

Feeling numb, needing coffee, I got up and moved over to the next mattress, separated by a table, on which Cynthia had been sleeping, the shape of her long smooth body still imprinted on the sheets. The moment my hands touched her she awoke and murmured, "Lion man."

I hadn't shaved; my hair had grown long and scraggly. She gazed up at me with her luminous blue-gray eyes. She looked at me for a long time, closed her eyes again, turned over, rolled back, stared at me piercingly, smiled gently, and said, "Ahhh, hello. *Bonjour, bonjour chérie*, my darling sweet shaggy man!"

She bounded to her feet, stretched to touch the tall green plants growing near the windowsill, and sang, "Good morning *chérie* baby, good morning sweety-pie, welcome, welcome ..."

I grabbed Cynthia hard from behind, trying to respond to her welcome.

She slipped away. "Hey, you big fish, can't you embrace me with—"

I pressed my lips against her pale, now wistful mouth. "Mmmm," she went with shivery ambiguity, "mmmmm."

This didn't satisfy me. "What does it mean, your 'mmmm'?" I asked.

"I don't know, it's hard for me to respond."

Encircling her with my arms, I pressed up against her small, pear-like breasts. When asleep, she had been lying with her long, languid buttocks nested against me, my knee wedged between her legs close to her pale tufted crevice. Now she pushed me down and lay on top of me, her head on my shoulder, her hair spilling in coils around my neck. She kissed me softly in silence.

"I love you but I can never belong to you. You know that by now, don't you?"

"I don't know anything about love," I said. I felt an urge to scream. "No, god-damn it, I don't know anything about love—zero, *rien*, *nada*, nothing! Help me! Explain it!"

Unexpectedly, she started to cry. She hugged me. There was a warm silence, underscored by a tender embrace. The oxidized silver Paris light swept over the tables and wicker chairs and came to a sudden stop in an oblong shape against the bathroom door. My eyes wandered over the big studio, the Giacometti-like paintings and drawings of herself Charlie had given her, the saffron-tinted curtains, the massive steel door (for protection), the dirty saucers on the windowsill for the neighborhood cats that came and went, Cynthia's frail shiny clothes flung over the shadowy chair, her suitcase ready for the next departure cracked open on the floor.

"What are you thinking of?" I asked.

"I'm thinking about this room, about you and me, how we fit into the room, and how we are in Paris, but how for us this room is really Paris, and if God's big eyes were looking down at us from the height of the ceiling, wouldn't we look so weird, lying embraced wrapped together so far below, and he would think, this has nothing to do with Paris, it could just as well be Ethiopia."

"Are you thinking about anything else?"

"I'm thinking about my dancing lesson this afternoon, and how I love to move, and how I want to be happy and enjoy life and especially not hurt you."

"I don't want you to think about that."

"But you asked me what I was thinking about. Don't worry what I was thinking about. It was nothing, just nothing. I was thinking without really thinking any thoughts about what I was thinking, negative or positive. They were just electrical impulses moving through my head. I never judge what I'm thinking about, do you?" she questioned.

I didn't answer but thrust my head between her long cool legs and tried to pry them open, first kissing the inside of her thighs, then gently nudging them apart. But she wriggled away.

"I'm going to take a bath."

"But we haven't even made love!"

"We can make love later when I'm clean and feeling better and washed and fresh."

She rose and donned a white silk, flower-embroidered robe she had found at the flea market at the Porte de Vanves. The light had changed, had become darker, like tarnished silver, elusive. She pranced on tiptoe through its shifting patterns that emerged under the wicker chairs Cynthia said were made by French prisoners and cost only forty francs each.

Paris was an exotic desert, and there was one person in that desert who mattered to me, but I knew in my heart and with all my feeling that I was about to lose her for reasons that neither she nor I could do anything about. That is why we rarely talked about the future, or, when we did, it was in the most casual disconnected way, as if what happened later would never be of any concern to us. We were living now, and Cynthia was the priestess of the moment—a complex and fragile being—and I was her Egyptian scribe and observer.

She sat in the small, pink, half-size bathtub. To fit, she had to pull her knees up to her breasts. She was reading a paperback by R.D. Laing, *The Politics of Experience*. I lit a Gitane cigarette and lay on the mattress, my hands behind my head, and stared at the spidery cracks on the ceiling. After a while she came out of the bathtub, a Ritz Hotel towel loosely wrapped around her waist. Still wet, she stood in the middle of the room, leafing through the Laing book, totally absorbed by it. Then she started to talk in a hushed pained voice about alienation and how strange and foreign the book made her feel, reminding her of all the terrible dislocations of her childhood, and how she knew she could never go back (to that place of her past) ever again.

Once we had been having lunch on a café terrace, and a group of American ladies recognized Cynthia from some recent fashion photos she had done. They came up to her and started babbling, but Cynthia cut them short, putting her arm around me, and saying, "Guess what, this is my husband, and we were just married and really want to be alone!"

Later, when I asked her what had prompted her to tell a lie like that, she said, "Because those silly women looked like they needed to hear it. It means nothing … you and I don't need anything between us. That's what's so beautiful—we don't need anything written between us, do we?"

Cynthia had a complex relationship with clothes. Although she made a living out of modeling them, she would buy them only when she could find them by chance, and when they cost next to nothing. When she had to wear them for her work, she said she hated them.

"I love to be nude and natural," she said. "If I could get away with wearing no clothes, I would."

She loved to playfully assume ballet dancer's positions. She would toy with and mock the idea of her own lightness, grace, and fragility.

In serious moments she told me, "I've already lost so much, my life is built on what I've lost. If I'm surviving, it's thanks to a system of loss."

Her sister had died in a car accident when Cynthia was six years old. Her father had died from some cancer contracted during his long hours in a paper pulp mill. Her mother had raised her as best she could in a remote town in the mountains of northern New Hampshire.

CHAPTER 24

▼

Years later I would remember all the precious moments spent with Cynthia.

I remembered her saying in her small, clear voice, "Life's haunted, like a house. Who cares about the past, all the phantoms? We have to live, what counts is the *now*."

We were walking on the *quais* along the Seine. It was August again; Paris was empty, light reflecting off the water in rows of ripples and haze, shuffling the identities of the old time-faithful monuments.

"You know what?" she said. "When you were inside me last night, I felt like I was absorbed by a thousand invisible little men, all pulling at me and tearing in all directions!"

"And then?"

"And then when you came I felt I was bonded with you, sharing your thoughts and feelings even more than yourself. But when I woke up, I was screaming, 'I can't take it! I can't take it!'"

"That's so weird. Why do you think that was?"

"I don't know," she murmured, hesitating. "I never told you, but when I first got to Paris, I was staying in this fifth-floor walk-up on rue Jacob, and one after-noon, when I was napping, this Arab guy I had seen in the neighborhood pushed open the door, which I hadn't locked. He had a knife. He ordered me to lie face-down on the bed and not to move. He started pulling off my pants. I was so frightened … he almost raped me. But at the last moment he heard some noises on the stairs and fled."

We had stopped in the middle of the Pont Neuf. The Seine waters swirled darkly below. Behind us the imposing mass of Notre Dame cathedral soared.

"I've lived a little more than twenty years." She started to cry, hugging me strongly, pressing her head wildly into my shoulders, as if to bury herself in them. "And nothing was good until I came to Paris and met you."

"Yes," I said, "and we're together and we have this and no one can ever take it away from us no matter what happens, right?"

"But it makes me sometimes so—" her voice broke.

I reached out to enfold her in my arms, to calm her, but she sprinted away to the end of the bridge. We dashed into a café. It was cool and dark. She ordered a *diabolo menthe*. I had a *citron pressé* followed by a *demi*.

"After the experience with that Arab guy, I just can't trust men any more. And I have this constant nightmare, that I'm coming home and a man is following me up the stairs, and he's big and strong, and I recognize him and tell him to stop but he just keeps coming after me—"

"Wow, that's really scary."

"But it doesn't even scare me," she said. "What scares me now is my absence of feeling, the absence of anything that scares me."

I yielded to a sudden desire and grabbed her and drew her to me, sliding my fingers to the inside of her thighs. But she caught my hand and moved it away gently.

"Just think," she said. "People are getting raped and murdered every minute everywhere. There's so much noise and violence and craziness. And here are you and I just living in this big glass bubble of you and me."

"But that's all there is, dear Cynthia," I said. "Just you and me."

"No, you're wrong, quite wrong," she answered quickly. "I'm only truly happy when I'm free."

"But what's freedom then?"

"It's being able to do anything as long as you don't hurt anyone."

"That's all well and good in theory. But suppose you're hurting me right now?" I found myself saying, and immediately regretted it.

"Why?" she replied sharply. "Because of your refusal to accept me truly as I am? You always want more!"

"Oh, come on, you've got to be kidding."

She shook her head. "No, I've always expected a lot of those I love." She sipped her green mint drink. "Give me a cigarette."

I bought a pack of Winstons and lit one for her. She rarely smoked.

"I don't know if I can be responsible for someone else any more. Right now I want to try just being responsible for myself and then we'll see what happens.

"But what about the idea of getting married?" I wondered. "You were the one who—"

"Did you know there's a Japanese custom—when he gets ready to marry, the man has the choice of choosing his sister spirit, his double, or his opposite. It's a choice every man has to face. Are you sure you really know what you want?"

"Ah, so! Ah, so! Now I understand!" I joked.

"Look, I'm happy to give you what I can give you, but I just don't know how long it will last," she concluded. "I may not even have enough to give. I may have to go elsewhere."

"I should write a song about you, 'Forever Elsewhere,'" I teased, signaling for the check.

"I'm a wanderer, you're not. Who knows whether we're truly good for each other? You're always trying to interpret things, fit them into your meaning. It's actually quite absurd. Me, I want nothing but the present, the moment, the gesture—nothing but gestures from now on, dance, motion, movement!" Simultaneously Cynthia shrugged and smiled, as if there were nothing more to say.

We left the café and strolled down the boulevard Saint-Michel, Cynthia, as usual, leaping on and off the benches by the bus stops. We crossed through the lovely place de Fürstenberg, where she once had taken me to see Delacroix's studio. "I want to show you his color, fire, imagination," she had said. "In Paris there is only gray. What good does gray do? I want the romantic heart, which gives me nourishment."

Back in the apartment, she became tense, nervously alert, like an animal at bay, not letting me come near her, not letting herself be touched. She sat in a corner of the alcove on a Moroccan cushion, her legs crossed, smoking one Winston after another.

I was thinking, *The power of what I feel for her is too precious to let myself be shaken by her refusals.*

But when Cynthia stubbornly repeated later that she did not want to come to bed with me, that she would sleep on the cushions because she needed to be by herself, I lost my control and shouted, "Well, you know what, damn you? You're even looking ugly right now!"

"That's what you think, fine!" she fought back. "Frankly, I don't give a fig how I look any more. You just want a woman to be in your image as a stupid man was created in the image of God. Well, I've had enough of your vanities! I don't want to hurt you by saying no to you, but I just don't want to be with you tonight. I need to be alone for my health and to think about things."

"Just let me lie next to you," I pleaded. "Just let me hold you and caress you and everything will be fine again."

"No, I can't, I really can't. And don't be so anguished! Just look at your face in the mirror and see what this is doing to you."

While I knew exactly what she was doing in putting me off, the yearning and desire for this young woman I needed but could not succeed in possessing rose up in me stronger than ever. If I cannot live in love, I thought, at least let me live outside of love, without the pain. Yet I could not relax enough to live in the present and make the moment the measure of man as Cynthia did. My thoughts relentlessly moved between the past, the future, what had not been, what might be, what could not be any longer. What I resolved was to try to be less possessive and demanding; I would try to adapt to her search for "different ways of being."

"Always touch your skin," Cynthia said, smoothing some tendrils of hair away from her forehead. "Only skin is real."

"Do you know that, since we ran into each other at that elevator at American Express, I've never stopped loving you?"

But she wondered, "Were Adam and Eve kicked out of paradise because they failed to live well together? How can you live with someone else and be true?" And once again she reminded me of Ode's "law of three nights."

"But I don't give a damn about those three nights," I replied sharply. "They were great, but they're gone. What I want to know now is what's going to happen with all the other nights?"

"The fourth night!" she laughed. "It could be a long one!"

What was I able to give her? Whatever it was, Cynthia was absolutely convinced there was "more" to be found. The key to the sweet dream—the "open sesame" to the realm of endless possibilities—was hidden in order to be found.

At other times, as quickly as the zinc-gray clouds scuttled low across the Paris skyline, she would slip into sadness and say, "The more I go, the more I live, the more I find there's less and less, and everything just keeps diminishing, until finally there's nothing left at all."

CHAPTER 25

▼

Much to my dismay, Cynthia started seeing a lot of Charlie again. There were those who thought Charlie was a great American artist; others said his work was too much in the shadow of his friend, Alberto Giacometti. Cynthia said she just liked his company because he did not "judge" her. Yet she would also joke about him and call him a "dinosaur, a prehistoric creature, something almost extinct."

On Saturday mornings she would go to Charlie's studio near the porte d'Orléans to pose for him. He had her sit nude on a chair near an old wood-burning stove. Furiously he would sketch her over and over again, as if trying to capture some abstract essence or decanted image of Cynthia.

Charlie said, "When I paint, I bring forth something inside myself that I didn't know was there. The point is to show how difficult it is to be alone, but how essential it is to be alone also. When I paint, I become me. That's who I am, in my paintings. Outside of my paintings, my 'self' doesn't exist. So I have to paint in order to be, and that's why I do it—because if I couldn't do it, I wouldn't be."

I certainly wasn't happy about these visits. How could I trust the relationship I sensed was again developing between Charlie and her? "When he's done with you," I warned her, "there'll be nothing left but your two eyes and your bones!"

"Yes, when at last there's nothing at all, then I'll be free!"

"No, you'll be reduced to just another one of his dark, fiery images. That's got nothing to do with you, Cynthia, that isn't you!"

"Do you know what you mean? Do you have any idea of the real me?"

"It's just his idea of you anyway, isn't it now?"

"I'm sick of talking this way," she snapped back.

"Right, why can't we just love each other like we once did?"

"Oh, yes, right, making love with you is the solution to all the problems, always!"

"Cynthia, please, I just want to try to find a way to keep us going forward."

"Then you've got to get rid of all your baggage from the past. Life's not just another bitter-sweet love song, you know."

"You know very well how far I've come, Cynthia. Don't you say that to me," I muttered angrily.

"Look, I want to keep going forward too. I'm just going to keep putting one dancing foot in front of another until I flop and drop." She sighed.

It was true: I felt I had outdistanced so many things. Even Cynthia—she was important to me, but, at the same time, I felt I had learned how to be truly alone.

As if she were thinking my thoughts, she said suddenly, "Do you know what really alone means? Can you even guess?"

"With all the time you're spending with Charlie these days," I said tartly, "you're making me learn."

"Too bad they never taught that kind of thing in school. It would come in handy."

I would realize later how much I was just trying to hang on to her, not to lose Cynthia.

On Sunday afternoons she would say, "Let's take one of those silly green buses where we can stand in the open air on the platform in the back and find out where Paris ends and where the country begins—the exact spot! We'll stop there. Surely there will be a mysterious café no one knows about. We'll rent a cheap room above it for a few hours and we'll make love anonymously, without names, as if we had just met each other, and weren't sure we'd ever see each other again."

Once, when we were on the bus near St-Germain-des-Prés, a man in blue dungarees and with a crazy moustache came riding along on a high bicycle and started waving at her. Amazingly, she knew who he was. "That's Jean. He works in a big French advertising agency. Once he cornered me in his apartment and tried to make love to me, but I escaped through a window in the bathroom."

That memory must have made her feel bold and sure of herself because she said, "I feel ready to do anything now. Everything's possible."

"Be careful. There's always a point of no return, a place from which you don't—and can't—come back."

"And is that place Paris for you?" she questioned. "Oh, dear you, I know it is and it doesn't make any difference to me, can't you know that?"

She seized my hand. "You know what? We're going to get there, where we've never been before, I promise you."

"You've got to be courageous to do that."

"Courage is a thing that, when you're as desperate as I am, comes rather easily."

Her moods were not always euphoric. Sometimes she would come back from her photo work and collapse on the pink pillows in her "Moroccan alcove." I would sit patiently and watch her, wondering what was this strange thing that made me feel that I loved her? When she played her flute, she would remind me, especially when seated cross-legged on the oriental cushions in the pink alcove, of a figure out of a Matisse painting.

CHAPTER 26

▼

It was autumn again, the most beautiful time in Paris. I had been in Paris now for much longer than I had ever planned. I had come for a few days and had stayed for more than a few years.

Outside, like a popular song, the September sun sang in the street. The loft-style apartment I now had was luminous, creamy. In the *boulangerie* next door, the woman selling fresh almond croissants and warm baguettes now knew me well. When I carried the long sticks of bread back in the morning, she would say, "That means the beautiful American girl is still with you, *non?*"

Yet despite the fact that Cynthia was now living with me, I still had the ineradicable feeling that she was a stranger to me.

Over the morning *café au lait*, "How old do you feel, Cynthia?" I asked her.

She smiled. "About old enough to want to crawl into something and hide for a long time. Either one or a hundred, I guess …" She laughed self-mockingly. She lay sideways on the bed, shy, sweet, nude.

"You don't have to be with me if you don't want," she mused. "You know, there's no obligation."

I didn't answer. I circled around her like a panther, making animal sounds, wooing her with my noises, something avid and powerful stirring inside me. "You still get this desire going so easily in me," I said.

Autumn in Paris, she said, the change of seasons, made her feel moody, vaguely pessimistic. "I try to say to myself that I know myself, that I know you, but no, there's no proof, is there?"

I squatted and looked intently at her. Fine hair, twisted in the form of shadowy gold grass, lay folded against the inside of her thighs. I longed to penetrate to the "core being" of Cynthia, to touch the essential mystery I was sure was enshrined there.

It was so taut, painful and tender, the silent understanding that could come suddenly at the end of a morning, with the strong yellow light drifting outside, the smell of chestnuts in the air, the slated apartment buildings reflected through the long windows on the blue asphalt.

In the loft upstairs, reached by a spiral staircase, Cynthia crouched on the pink velvet cushions she had sewn. She stiffened her shoulders, crossed her legs, bent her forearms, locked her hands on her hips, then, keeping her back straight, she arched up and down, breathing deeply. Finally she slipped into a lotus position and into a deep meditative state.

She remained immobile for a long time, breathing slowly, sinking so far into herself that she became inaccessible.

After a while, her serene immobility became unbearable to me. I came up behind her and whispered, "Cynthia, I need to know if you love me, if you have any feeling for me at all."

She didn't answer. She stood up, calmly removed her clothes, and climbed into the small, curved bathtub. Relaxing, she settled back, letting the water run over her shoulders. She looked at me curiously, as if I were a foreigner, and said, "What are you watching me for?"

"I'm so stupid," I said. "I don't know anything about you. Really, I don't even know why I'm here."

She stood up, her back turned to me, started drying herself. My eyes followed the slender streaming shape of her haunches, which looked like an urn with a golden cleft.

She looked at me, frowning slightly. "Do you mind if I ask you a personal question?"

"No, go ahead."

"You're a Scorpio, aren't you?"

"Yes."

"That means you take love too seriously. You should take it playfully, joyously."

"And how do I take it?"

"You know what I'd like to do?" she asked brightly, abruptly changing the subject. "Be in the circus. I'd love to trip and flap and flip and flop and fall all over my feet. I'd love to be in a place where it would be normal for seals to ride on the backs of horses."

Cynthia had put on a striped Japanese gown, a *yukata*.

Seized with sudden desire for her, I put my hands on her shoulders, felt the fresh bathed warmth of her skin, drew her powerfully to me.

She laughed and skipped away. "I don't know if I'm ready for that now!"

Her refusal hurt me, but I didn't say anything. The fact that we had made love many times before didn't count. She applied a strict existential logic: this was a new moment, a curtain was dropped forever on the past.

The duplex apartment we shared was near the Montparnasse cemetery. It was beautiful, with a sweeping view through the large windows of the close-cropped plane trees below and the cold gravestones. A grayish silver light floated over everything. I tried to adapt to this new style of life that seemed to have no future and no past but hung as if suspended in an ever-expanding *now*. Cynthia put a single mattress on the floor and insisted on sleeping there. After all the time she had spent in Morocco, she had become so used to living near the ground that she did not like beds any more. We still made love, but she would be passive, not fully participating. She explained she felt distracted because she still had strong feelings for Charlie. I would lie next to her as she retreated into the haven of her mattress, closing my arms protectively around her. She wouldn't say anything, she would lie very still, breathing slowly in and out.

I kept trying to analyze what was the power that drew me to her.

One October night I knelt next to her. Hunched above her, with a cool quiet tenderness I whispered, "Cynthia, if you should go away again, I don't know what I would do, I don't know how I could live."

She surprised me, turning suddenly toward me, a strange half-smile on her face. Her moist gray-blue eyes grew very wide.

"But it's very possible that I might leave. It could happen at any time."

"That would just kill me," I groaned.

"No, it won't. You're too attached to me. You think you've found something, but you really haven't found anything. I'm nothing. I just reflect what you are."

"Don't talk such nonsense."

"But it's true!"

I hugged her, kissing her softly on her neck, behind her ears, in the shallows of her pale shoulders.

"Say you won't leave me, Cynthia. Don't do it. We can stay in Paris. We can build a life together."

She shook her head. She seemed dazed. "No, no, let's not. Let's just be together now."

She pulled me down to her on the narrow mattress. Shadows from the street spilled over our bodies.

"Come on top of me." She was lying on her haunches, soft, fragile, exposed.

I towered above her, then dug down, hard and jabbing, trying to thrust myself as far into her as possible. Gasping, our twin flesh buttoned together, we became one as the words in a poem are one.

Cynthia was laughing now, giggling, she prodded me, pressing her nails down sharply into the back of my shuddering shoulders. "Ah, sock it to me, baby!" she cried out.

In that late autumn, Paris had a harsh, decisive clarity. The light falling through the wide windows of our studio loft was the color of silver apples. I knew that I was in love with her, that Cynthia and Paris were inextricably mingled together, that I would not be able to leave one or the other as long as this wave of generous feeling continued.

"So here we are, another morning in gay Paree!" she announced.

The early morning street noises had already subsided. Another day like a blank canvas stretched in front of us. I opened my eyes and looked up slowly.

She was watching me, looking down. "You smell of pine wood."

Instinctively I reached out for her but she resisted. It was her special way to tease me, to be at once with me and not with me—present yet absent at the same time.

Over an espresso with a single sugar cube, she remarked, "Did you know the Turks have a custom of hanging above their kids' beds a life-size, full-length portrait of the child. Very strange. Can you remember the first experience of looking at yourself in the mirror as a child? It's a really important and traumatic moment."

I could not remember much about my childhood. It had been so awful I had chosen to eliminate it from my conscious life.

"I still can remember what it was like to be a child," she went on. "I slip in and out of those memories quite often. Sometimes I feel I am a child and wonder how I'm ever going to return to the adult world. The child—to become like a child again, to see everything as new, wondrous."

"I guess I've just fallen in love with a child-woman."

"I'm going back to bed," she changed the subject. "That party last night, all the champagne, gave me a headache. I'm going to have a *grasse matinée*, a lazy-bones morning."

The evening before we had gone to a *nuit blanche soirée poetique* in a twelve-bedroom apartment on the Île Saint-Louis that belonged to the owner of a legendary champagne factory. Bottles of his champagne had floated amid huge blocks of ice in all the bathtubs and sinks.

"Hey," I called over to her, alarmed "I think your goldfish Souki is dead."

"No, not Souki, no, that can't be."

"Come and look."

The shiny red fish she called Souki dangled motionlessly against the brightly colored pebbles at the bottom of the fish bowl.

"Maybe she ate too much," Cynthia said. "I wanted her to be happy so last night I gave her a feast of French bread. Shake the bowl. See if she floats."

I gripped the dumb bowl and shook it harder and harder, the water sloshing as I tried to waken her goldfish. But Souki didn't move.

"Go bury her in the green plant pot."

When I came back from the burial, Cynthia said, "Here, I have a present for you."

It was a crayon drawing she had just done entitled "Multiple Phantoms." It was filled with mad moons, goldfish stars, airborne lovers, haunting, spectral forms, and, balanced on top of a pyramid, an all-observing Egyptian eye.

Souki's death had made Cynthia moody. "It's a bad sign," she said. "Would you make me another espresso?"

She was wearing an iris-blue nightgown that clung supplely to her body. When she saw me come out of the kitchen carrying, on a lacquered Japanese tray, the espresso coffee I had just made, she burst out laughing, her laughter vibrant and wild.

"What so funny, honey?"

"Because I can still say yes to you, my great shaggy lion, my love. You make me feel so wonderful."

Her words were precious to me. I put the tray down and huffed and swaggered around her like some clumsy, love-stricken beast.

She reached down, grabbed a shock of my long hair, and pulled me to her. "Come, my love. Come, my life," she whispered.

She smiled broadly. She was now nude, offered, and open.

I went down with my head, advancing toward her.

"*Touchez pas, touchez pas,*" she warned.

Before I could react, she caressed my forehead, then suddenly dropped her hands between my thighs and seized my rising sex.

"Let me see that thing of yours, that crazy thing, that 'thump thump'!"

I throbbed with her promises. She then let me penetrate her half-opened, avocado-smooth mouth. I was grateful and knew that making love together would be very beautiful and warm and full of promise and new life, as when you take your first bath after a week of rain and cold.

At night she insisted on sleeping on her mattress on the floor and would say, "*Bonne nuit*, baby. Goodnight, my sweet *chérie* darling." Sometimes, before the first light broke, she would spring onto my bed, rolling her svelte body on top of me, fondling me playfully. "Where's that thing of yours?" she would ask. "Your rose *truc*? I want to see him, that big 'thump thump'!"

Her vital frivolity excited me, but I could not help wondering whether we were simply trapped in a present that meant nothing, playing a game without consequences, a theatre of passion that, at best, showed the last traces of love.

"You take everything too seriously," she admonished. "You're too tough, too hard. I'm just trying to soften you up."

At other times I would approach her just as she was emerging from her sleep, pressing against her transparent skin, her warm, furred body. I would lean over her, looking at her as if to decipher her. With the intensity of a sentinel, I would watch her, searching for a sign in her clear large luminous eyes.

"*Bonjour*, 'thump thump,'" she murmured.

Was her taunting inaccessibility a test, a way of forcing me to live beyond myself and my natural instincts?

Unable to control the urge to possess her, I eventually worked myself into the pale gold target between her legs, losing myself in the unconscious feeling of pure desire.

But Cynthia escaped to some abstract zone. In order to save herself, did she have to ignore me? But in order to feel myself as real, I felt I had to go deeper inside her. She floated, serenely absent, as if detached from her body. Just at the moment when I surged over the climax barrier, I popped my eyes open wide and stared down at her. She winked. It was quick, a flash, but an unmistakable wink.

CHAPTER 27

▼

For a brief interval it seemed that we shared a new tender gentleness and sensual understanding. Cynthia stayed with me. She seemed submerged within herself or within the confines of our physical relationship. "I'm not interested in love, only in the proofs of love," she stated.

She liked to sit very still on the cushions in her Moroccan-style alcove. Sometimes Japanese or Arab friends would come to visit. They would sit around in a circle speaking in low voices. Cynthia would bring out the silver-engraved, water-cooled pipe, a gift from Ode, and they would smoke. Once Cynthia made hashish crepes. They tasted good; everyone liked them.

Outside the air had a luminous, cold clarity. It was the first of November, the Day of the Dead.

"I feel all these changes inside me," she said. "I should know myself by now. I certainly should know you, but no, there's no proof."

"How can you say that, especially after making love like we did last night?"

"Yes, even after we made love like that."

I sat and observed her. She was lying semi-nude on the black leather sofa. A shadow lightly veiled the wedge of her sex. I realized I had only touched her flesh, had not yet succeeded in penetrating to the heart of her.

"Let's talk about our relationship then," I said. "Let's be honest about our feelings."

For some reason that made her angry. "Damn! Is that all you can do, analyze your feelings?"

"Okay, here it is," I said. "Answer me: do you still love me or not?"

She didn't answer me. She removed her wrap and climbed into the half-size tub. "Come sit with me."

I sat stupidly on the edge of the bathtub, watching her again go through her ritual ablutions. I watched the water trickling over her small, sharply pointed breasts.

"If you want to live with me, you cannot make love to me just because I am here and you think I belong to you. You must be gentle with me and give me time."

"But it's not as if we just met each other!" I laughed bitterly.

"I'm so very tired," she sighed, rising from her bath. "I'm going to take a siesta on those cushions. It's good to be close to the ground."

I knelt next to her, watching her slumber, inhaling her body's perfume, listening to the even rise and fall of her breath.

When she finally stirred she found me leaning over her. With a cool, quiet tenderness, I whispered, "Cynthia, I need you. If you should ever leave me again, I would go crazy."

She surprised me with a smile, her moist, gray blue eyes growing even wider. "But did you ever think, it's very possible that I might die?"

"That's ridiculous!" I exclaimed.

"No, it isn't. It's true," she repeated with a dull insistency that stunned me.

I recalled a few of the crazy words she had murmured once before—her clear laughter, then the sudden, startlingly grave way in which she had pronounced, "I know that I'm going to kill myself."

"How strange! How frightening! Who told you that?"

"No one told me that. No one at all."

"Then how or why do you think you're going to kill yourself?"

"Because I want to die by my own hand," she responded simply. "It's the only way to die. It's the nearest one can come to being actually conscious of one's own death."

"And when are you going to do this?" I pursued what I felt was an absurd game.

"When I feel the right moment. I feel as if I'm already old, my body already betraying me."

She seized my head and pulled it against her pear-shaped breasts. "If ever things become really desperate for you, think of me. I do love you, *tu sais*, you know. Remember that, whatever happens."

CHAPTER 28

▼

We were going out with Jean-François, the publisher of the hip monthly magazine *The Underground Sun*, and with Judy, whom he had recently married. Judy came from Virginia and, like Cynthia, had arrived in Paris when she was nineteen to study for a year at the American University in Paris. When she met Jean-François, her life took another direction. She joked how Jean-François at first had refused to buy any American products for her—even cornflakes—on the grounds that "it helped the American economy and, by extension, the American involvement in Vietnam." Furious, one day she decided she had had enough. She packed all his bags, threw them on the street, and locked the door. He threatened to kill her if she did not take him back. Instead, he finally bought the apartment and married her.

"Of course I don't sleep with Jean-François any more," Judy was quick to tell anyone who would listen. "He's so busy with his magazine and all his French flirts. He says he loves me, but he doesn't pay attention to me, and, oh my God, I'm just so horny! He tells me this is France, I can do anything I want, but you know what? The moment he says that, somehow I don't care so much. How do you manage?"

"When I'm with a man I love, or think I love, then I always have a difficult time," Cynthia said. "When there are other, more casual encounters, then it's easier for me to forget myself, to be more sensual, complete, and free."

"When I first met Jean-François," Judy went on, "if I didn't make love at least once a day, I would feel sick. But now Jean-François is always going off to his political meetings."

Jean-François had another point of view. He put it this way to me, "With all the critical things going on in the world, the most important thing for a man today is whether he can contribute, play a role. There's no middle ground. He's got to engage himself. If he's just going to sit on the sidelines and observe, why *merde* [shit], he can go to hell! Everything's political. Since you can't escape, you must act. We all undergo the effects of politics in our daily lives. We must react. Yesterday I went to an anti-Vietnam war demonstration in front of the American Embassy. The place was crawling with *flics* [cops], but it was great, we made our point."

"Yes, exactly," Cynthia chimed in with enthusiasm. "The most important thing today is finding new ways to live. Certainly all the old ways have failed. Bankruptcy. Why do you think so many of our friends go off on trips to Morocco or India? Because words have failed and they want to re-invent themselves in a new space and geography, to create a new language."

It all sounded great, I thought, but why was it that even Cynthia and I were so torn apart in our ways of living, of loving? Why did she keep telling me that divided thinking was foreign to her and she wanted to go someplace where she could find spontaneity and equilibrium?

We went for a walk along the long shadowy alleys of the Luxembourg gardens. At a kiosk on the corner of the Boulevard Saint-Michel, she stopped to leaf through the latest *Paris Fashion* magazine in which there were some glamorous photos of her. She wore clothes so naturally, as if they were part of her being. Her blonde hair shone brightly, her gray-blue eyes were bright, and I couldn't help thinking: Cynthia is nothing but brightness.

Under the chestnut trees along the geometric paths of the garden, some children were burying a lizard. "Look," she said excitedly. "Do you see how they've dug a magic circle in the ground and planted it with tiny crosses? Watch their eyes. It's only a lizard, but it's as if the death of the whole universe were passing in front of them."

CHAPTER 29

▼

December came, and through a girl we knew slightly called Sophia, we were invited to a "Scorpio party." When we arrived, a bouquet of roses was presented to me. "Because you're a Scorpio," the hostess said. "Everyone who's a Scorpio gets roses."

It was a typical Parisian high-fashion party, thronged with many rich, crazy people. There was Roederer crystal champagne to drink and peppered vodka. Salmon eggs and caviar were served at midnight. Mme. Lalou, the hostess, told me she kept a gallery below her apartment as a *caprice* and because she loved Sophia's artwork.

Garbed in a shimmering gown of gray-white satin, Sophia moved nimbly among the guests. In a mincing, softly provocative voice, she told me this party was also being given in honor of her work. Her paintings depicted bright, fluttery fragments of blue-and-white bodies, their buttocks patterned with multicolored butterflies.

"Why do you stay with that American girl?" Sophia asked me. "Come with me and I will show you many new things!"

Next to me was a slim-hipped young man with a shock of red hair. "That's Frederick. He's Mme. Lalou's lover," Sophie whispered to me. "And of some other rich ladies as well."

My eyes were on Cynthia, who looked more beautiful than ever that evening. She had star powder on her eyelids, and she danced and mocked those around her with poetry and joyous wit.

"She looks like she stepped straight out of an F. Scott Fitzgerald book," someone commented.

A heavy-set, flat-footed man approached Cynthia, stared down at her as if trying to figure her out, and then proclaimed proudly, "I am a banker from Cairo!"

Cynthia shook her bare shoulders at him, did an imitation Marilyn "pout," then frowned at him in disapproval with lowered eyebrows.

The fat banker groaned and bobbled away, lost in the bustling crowd.

Another group was animatedly discussing astrological signs. "Don't you think," they asked me, "that the Scorpio is the most sensual, intelligent sign?"

"Bullshit," I said.

"Tell us what it's like to be an American Scorpio," someone suggested, and they all clamored.

Suddenly Cynthia appeared and sang in French, *"Je bois de la liqueur, mais je fais le piqueur."* (I drink liquor but I sting.)

Everyone laughed.

"Drink some more peppered vodka and maybe you'll lose your nasty desire to sting," urged Mme. Lalou.

The Egyptian banker returned, swaying, obviously drunk. He grabbed Cynthia, tried to pull her to him. I saw how his round, stupidly cheerful, loose face had swollen.

As usual, Cynthia was letting herself go with the flow of the moment.

I felt I had to protect her. Picking up a heavy coffee-table book on Tantric art, I brought it down hard over the banker's head. He fell back stunned, gasping for air. A trail of blood appeared on his forehead. "You beast, you swine!" he cursed.

"You bad, mad, crazy American Scorpio!" someone else joined in.

"Let's get out of here," I told Cynthia, pulling her away.

"That banker reminded me of a lobster!" Cynthia said as we hailed a taxi and drove away along the Seine embankment. "I keep seeing him attacking me with those pincer arms of his."

Impulsively, she reached over and embraced me just as we swerved around the lighted obelisk in the center of the place de la Concorde.

"You know what?" she murmured. "I don't give a damn about anything, even about me. I just care about what happens between you and me tonight."

We got out of the cab near the Notre Dame cathedral, and I took her to a secret, magical place I knew along the river bank. There, on the cobbled pavement under the dark bridge arches, I caressed her for a long time and kissed her neck and her arms repeatedly. I pulled her warm body to me and felt her spirit for the first time truly fuse with mine, and I knew that we were as one. Against the outcropping stone, with the huge, velvety Paris night blanketed over us, and the river black and shiny with the reflected glow, I came up hard and was suddenly inside her yes-saying body. She said she wanted me too. She took me sweetly and violently, and it was good and true and lasted long.

CHAPTER 30

▼

After that evening I lived an absolute point of intensity. I felt a pure joy to know that with Cynthia life had begun again. It was good to know that our relationship had a renewed dynamic, that we were headed down a new and uncharted path.

A short time later Cynthia told me excitedly that she might be pregnant. She said she had an appointment at the American Hospital to confirm the results.

I had hardly had time to analyze this new and potentially complex situation as well as my feelings toward fatherhood when Cynthia came rushing back into the apartment and shouted, "Guess what? I'm not pregnant!"

I felt inexplicably disappointed, as if something that was about to become rightfully mine had been taken away. When I joked that it was easy to try again, she answered firmly, "No ... I guess I feel relieved—you know, life is so terrible, stupid, why impose that burden on another being?"

Cynthia then decided she had to get rid of those old photographs she had done during her modeling days. Judy came and they spent a good afternoon rummaging around and collecting all the slick black-and-white images.

"I want to destroy everything," Cynthia announced. "I don't want any old images of myself lying around for someone else to use or exploit. I want to start from nothing, with a *tabula rasa*, a clean slate."

She was merciless in her choices, and every image from her past on that fateful day—the day I always remembered as the one where she found out she was not pregnant—was destroyed.

She brooded, retreated to her alcove, sat for hours in a meditative position, or played wistful melodies on her silver flute.

Wanting to make it somehow good for her, I whooped and rushed after her. Leaping to the top of a table, I pretended to pounce on her. But she deftly eluded me, then counter-attacked, dashing around the big gray room, laughing and shouting, trying to grab me and hold me however she could, seizing my swollen penis and playfully tugging at it.

"Okay, let's do it, let's do it!" I yelled, doubled over.

Her graceful fingers stabbed at my belly again. She seized the back of my head, tugging at my long hair. But when I responded by trying to hoist her in my arms and throw her on the bed, she checked me with a sharp, "Hey, wait. What are you doing?"

Impatient, excited now, I stomped around her. "Come on! Let's go! Let's do it now! I've got to find the gold buried inside you!"

Openly she mocked, "Yes, yes, you're so poor! If you don't touch me, you'll starve, you poor thing."

I managed to maneuver myself on top of her, but again she twisted aside. From a certain distance she eyed my coldly, objectively surveying my naked state.

"You're crazy," she said. "All you want to do is hump me, and the only reason you want me is because I don't let you do it as much as you want. But I don't care, I like you anyway, in spite of everything."

I cradled her in my arms; the half-light shone on her upturned face. We rocked back and forth holding each other gently in the shadows.

"*Je t'aime,* Cynthia. *Je t'aime,*" I murmured.

But feeling myself grow hard again, I started to tease her, almost brutally. "My dear, sweet girl, it's time now to really do it, to get the act on."

"You're so harsh!" she cried. And she rose and ran off, out of the apartment.

I stood shaking with pain. I felt ugly, thick, engorged with my own blood, not knowing what to do. The rapidity with which Cynthia could change amazed me. She had always had a strange habit of slipping away. Then suddenly she would turn to glimpse my face, to check my reaction, and try to lure me again to her.

I ran out onto the boulevard Montparnasse, which was astir with people and cars, and caught up with her. "I'm so sorry I was a little rough," I said. "But maybe if you could just relax, we could both be so happy."

"You know what? I don't think I've ever truly understood you," she answered.

That afternoon the late December sun had a mild metallic radiance to it. We walked back along the noisy boulevard.

"Can I look at your hands?" she asked.

"What for?" I wondered.

"I just want to see if they say anything special to me."

Later, when we were back in the apartment, I said, "Now it's my turn. I want to look at your breasts."

"Why?" she wondered out loud. "Who would ever want to look at me? Who? Who?"

CHAPTER 31

▼

I think it was about that time that Cynthia started seeing Charlie again. She said she felt drawn to him in a way that she could not explain. I let it happen because Charlie had become a friend and I never thought that he would be capable of betraying that friendship.

Charlie was an artist—the real thing—and he divided his time between Paris and New York. Always restless, driven by some demonic sense of "otherness," he needed to be always where he was not. He was almost bald, and his bullet-shaped head made him look even tougher, more intense. He had Picasso-dark eyes, a ready laugh, and polite but nervous gestures. I guessed Charlie must have been in his late sixties. He liked to joke that it was drinking a bottle of Johnny Walker a day that had kept him alive for so long.

In his Montparnasse studio he had a few paintings by Giacometti, some Matisse drawings, and a Cycladic "woman" sculpture he had purchased "for peanuts" during the war.

"You'll have to excuse me, I'm a little thirsty this morning," Charlie said, as the smooth scotch trickled over the tiny round ice cubes.

"I was born in Paris on All Saint's Day, November 1," he began. "My earliest memories were those of being offered presents in the morning, then in the afternoon being led by the hand, by my parents, to pay our respects to the dead in the cemetery. Ever since then I've been hoping I'll die on the Day of the Dead, so that my birthday would also be my death day. I guess that's why I've always hated any kind of gifts—gifts and flowers—they just remind me of death. And you know what's really strange? My father happened to die on November 1. So usually on that day I stay in bed, checking my pulse, making sure I'm alive!"

Charlie often wore dark glasses, and, with his black fedora hat, he resembled a real gangster. He moved nervously, talked quickly, sometimes mumbling, frequently repeating himself, as if trying to say something that finally could not be said. And he would draw constantly, sketching heads or the figures of nude women on the back of napkins, matchboxes, or any surface that was available

"During the Algerian war there were no materials available, so I would scribble or draw on anything I could get, even on packs of cigarettes. I've done a lot of work, but I haven't been able to keep much. I destroy a lot. I've learned one thing: it's useless to try to keep things when the real, essential things are always kept anyway."

Charlie shoved some wood into the potbellied stove that kept his studio somewhat warm in wintertime. Through the slanted roof windows the light came in clear and hard.

I had come to talk about Cynthia, but Charlie went on, "My father was French, my mother American. I have an American passport. I live in two places—New York, Paris. When I was younger I was just as crazy and revolutionary as any of you kids is today. I went to Spain, volunteered to fight in that Civil War. They asked me if I knew how to handle a machine gun. I said no. End of that. Now I like my silence, my solitude. I live simply, I draw, I paint. And I detest all these fake Rimbauds running around Paris. All these fake artists who think they know something because they've gone to art school. If you see a dog shitting in the street, you don't go up and say, 'Hello, Mr. Dog, I think you've just created a masterpiece!'"

"I can't paint all the time. There are only a few good moments anyway. So I have some spare time. Days that just pass by. A question of life and destruction. It's true I like to drink. Sometimes I think: if could find something to love …"

"When my father died he left me a small trust fund, so I've been living on that for years. Just enough to give me my freedom. What happens in the States is you get a lot of artists who have to become professors. That kills them. An artist, a musician, a poet, is the exact opposite of a professor."

"In Paris after the war I wanted to be a jazz musician, even played piano in some bars. But I knew I wasn't good enough. But I do know how to paint. Yet art for me is something that can never be completed, never truly finished. In the end you've got to go back to the figure, to a face, to a woman's sex. You need architecture and you need a body. First man makes a house. He puts up the walls, then he tries to find some way he can live in it, be happy in it. He starts painting his cave, like at Lascaux. But personal stories don't matter. I could never paint some of the things that happened to me; for example, when I was before a German firing squad. Today everyone has some story to tell. Why not just trust your memory?"

"What I lived in the war killed my hopes. Even the communists here don't accept me—they don't like pessimists. But how can you be an optimist today? It's clear the city of God will never be installed upon earth. That's a dream and I'm not a dreamer. I'm interested in only one thing: what happens when a man gets beyond politics, when his real freedom begins. There's no right or perfect moment for that. It can happen any time. Growth and freedom and death are always here on the same level, for he who knows how to see."

The afternoon brightened. Next to the gun-gray faucet in the studio corner, a single rose stem protruded from a Coca-Cola bottle. Charlie's paintings—huge, massive sketches of angular, nude women, their sexes lit as if on fire, depicted as if they were crucified on a vanishing chair or table—created a lucid somber mood.

"A man doesn't change," Charlie was saying. "You are what you are. And you know exactly what that is the instant you wake up in the morning or fall asleep at night."

The problem now was that Charlie had fallen in love with Cynthia. She had started coming to his studio again to pose for him. Gradually he had approached her and, no doubt, had tried to touch her. Whether she had yielded to him or not, I didn't know or care to know.

"I realize I can't keep her," Charlie said. "But I'm going to fight like hell for every moment of her that I can get.

"I've been moving around all my life. I've never stayed in one place for more than six months. My first wife set herself on fire in her New York City apartment and burned herself to death. After that I knew you have to keep on going, and it doesn't matter whether in the end there's victory or defeat. But every now and then you find like an inn, a bright spot, a resting place where you can live for a while. That's what I've found with Cynthia. She's like a patch of light, a grove of clarity, an opening. I can't let it go. I'm used to the darkness, I know what it is. I know how to live in my cave. I've been living in it a long time, and now I'm going to hold on to her as long as I can."

"But I love her too, Charlie," I said point-blank. "I came to Paris not expecting anything, but I met her and now I can't imagine my life without her."

"Let me tell you something: during the war, when we were all so poor and had nothing, I fell in love with this music teacher. She taught piano to kids and was crippled, couldn't walk by herself. She was very shy. It was fantastic—damn! To think that I lost track of her, never saw her again, and I didn't realize my feelings at the time, wasn't capable of even guessing ...! How I remember her standing on the doorstep sobbing, telling me things I didn't know how to understand. And, oh my god, my going away, not ever seeing her again, coming back after the war to find the house destroyed. But that moment with her I've always held on to, it's become so big in my memory—huge.

"That day I got onto an army truck," Charlie continued, "going to the front, the no man's land. German soldiers were patrolling it at irregular intervals. You didn't know when they would pass. You just had to run and take your chances. I met up with a young girl from the village. She said, 'Can I run with you?' I answered, 'Why not?' We started running across a charred field. There were three of us. That crazy girl had brought a heavy suitcase with her. She kept dropping and stumbling over it. I tried to carry it for her but couldn't. Finally I flung it away and said, 'Every man for himself.'

"We all ran like hell. The girl followed, still trying to drag her damn suitcase. We reached the other side of the field safely. It got dark. Now we were out of the danger zone, but we didn't have any papers. We went to a café, got something to eat. 'We'll go to the train station,' I said. 'Try to catch a train out.' The girl said, 'But what happens if we get picked up on the platform?' 'Just say we're tourists,' I told her. 'That we spent the night in the chateau of the Count nearby.' 'But what about my honor?' the girl asked. 'Better to lose your honor than your neck.' We went to the train station, stood on the platform holding hands like lovers. German soldiers passed. Nothing happened. Two trains came. I got on one, she got on the other. We went in opposite directions."

I told Charlie I had to go. I didn't want to listen to his stories any more. He was a man from a different generation, with completely different experiences. But there was one thing that bound us together: Cynthia.

As I was walking out into the dull leaden gray light of that November afternoon, Charlie grabbed me by the shoulder and said, "I always knew that if I ever found a woman whom I could truly love, and was worth loving, I would drop painting and everything else in a second. Well, kiddo, guess what? It's happened."

CHAPTER 32

▼

The evening was crisp, hard, with a faint fog in the street and the crowd fleeing like phantoms along the narrow sidewalk. A blind man was trying to buy a *baguette*—a stick of bread. Farther ahead, a young woman had propped her bicycle near a merry-go-round pole and was letting a man in a brown raincoat embrace her. Cynthia opened the door.

She seemed surprised to see me. "It's getting cold. I hate winter in Paris, it's so gray every day. My body feels dead."

In the Luxembourg gardens, the trees had long since shed their leaves. Even the chairs looked abandoned and dry. Cynthia said she wanted a *petit-crème*, and we went in search of a friendly café down those deep, once-golden alleys that had served as the backdrop to our happiness. Cynthia was smiling in a radiant way and she gripped me tightly, almost violently, against her fur coat in the damp electric mist. Running shadows of other couples and phantom lovers moved beside us.

"You look so happy," I said. "Are you in love with Charlie? Tell me, I have to know."

She stopped, paused. "I like him, but, to be honest, I'm not sure if I love him."

"But will you sleep with him again?"

"Maybe. Who knows?"

The pain cut through me, but I was thinking: for the rest of your life you will remember and cherish these moments.

We walked past the faded green horses in the fountain basin, forever frozen in their leaping stance of joy. There was the zinc smell of oysters being shucked from the restaurant La Closerie des Lilas on the corner.

Cynthia sensed my thoughts, jumped on them. "Life—*la vie*—what can we do but enjoy it?"

"But I worry about what's happening between us, about how I can keep you."

"There's nothing to worry about," she tried to reassure me. "I'm not afraid of anything that might happen, and I trust you."

A duo of Afghan hounds strolled by. One had one of its legs bandaged. A beautiful Greek woman was walking them. Cynthia said her name was Olga. She had lived some tragic misadventure, now she never opened her lips, never said a word, never received any visits, lived only for her two dogs.

In silence we went back to the apartment I had at the end of rue Campagne-lrè.

"You remember how you once told me you didn't believe in love but only in the proofs of love?" I asked.

"Yes, and so?"

"Well, if you love me, let's prove it—let's jump into bed."

"But—like that, right now?"

"Yes, Cynthia," I said. "I need to know you again. I need to know you're mine."

I grabbed her and lifted her up off the floor and swung her around.

"Let me go! Let me go!"

"I just want you to kiss me."

"That's all, enough, *c'est assez comme ça.*"

I bent her much-loved head back and kissed her a few times with brief but intense passion.

"You kiss me like a gangster!" she rebuked me. "Just kiss me softly. Don't think about anything else. Can't you just kiss me softly and tenderly?"

My lips met hers, clamped down hard on them, tasted them. My lips adhered to hers, clung to every moment of salty sweetness. Now she ran her fingers sensuously toward the base of my arched spine.

"Touch me, touch me," I urged her.

"I can't."

"Yes you can. Do it. Now."

"No, no, please no." She backed off. She moved away from me, her hips mesmerizing in retreat.

From somewhere out of the depths of herself, she groaned, "Oh, Charlie!"

"Fuck Charlie."

"Charlie's nice," she answered angrily. "And you should see him make love. For an old guy, he's quick as a monkey!"

I slapped her.

She was stunned. She revolted. "Don't you—!"

"Charlie's a no-good, dirty old man, a lecherous, alcoholic, antediluvian monster!"

"My, how good you are with words!" she burst out laughing.

I rolled my body toward her, now laughing too. Playfully, I began to sink my tongue into the hollows of her long neck.

"Get that snake, worm, out of here!" she cried, giggling.

I grabbed her hands and pinned them above her. Her back pressed against the high studio wall, she allowed me to rip off her blouse.

I suckled her breasts hungrily, driving one hand down between her legs and splitting them. Almost straddling me, and with a soft gasp, she let me enter her. Soon I was shaking in a series of spasmodic convulsions, which she seemed to share. Then she collapsed upon me, pulling me down, kissing me in a panic fashion, murmuring, "You're not so bad, you're not so bad! I still rather like you, I think."

I still felt drawn to her in a way that I could not explain. I would lie next to her and caress her cascading blonde hair for a long time without saying anything. Cynthia let me touch her without offering anything of herself. It was as if she kept her true energy, her central being, in reserve, to spring it loose unexpectedly at an opportune moment.

"Let's go for a walk in the Luxembourg gardens," she said. "Let's go there and see if any roses are by chance still alive."

The streaked silver light struck the old stone buildings. Blue and gray pigeons swarmed over the rooftops. Children played in the graveled alleys; their happy cries rose in the pale, muted air. It was true I had survived the test of the "law of three nights." Yet the equilibrium we had was so finely strung, delicately balanced, that I knew it could break without warning at any time.

CHAPTER 33

▼

Jean-François, Judy's husband, had asked me if I would help him with his project to convert an ex-bordello into a super-hip club. We went to visit the building. An old lady, who had just died, had lived alone in it for the last twenty years. It was a huge feudal house set back in the middle of a fashionable block. A stone portal and studded black doors made it invisible from the street. There was a garden with a labyrinth. There was a terrace, and there were tiny, hidden rooms and alcoves draped in red velvet. Gothic furniture and enormous art-nouveau mirrors fronted the vast curving staircase. Jean-François wanted to create an exclusive private club that would be a combination library, discotheque, massage and relaxation center, bar and restaurant. It would be a kind of "perpetual festival" where people "in the know" could get together to explore possibilities. Jean-François thought Ode would be the ideal manager for this "dynamic living centre."

"She has no emotions, no feelings. She would be the best one to deal with the desires of so many people."

In an antique keyhole desk, Cynthia found a packet of handwritten love letters that had been written in the late 1890s and wrapped with care in blue ribbon. "You know what I'm discovering?" she said as she perused them. "Love and sex are two completely different things. That is why I want to separate them and why I think I need two men in my life."

"Only two?" Jean-François joked.

"You're right. What about the spirit? I might need three."

"If you were an animal, you'd be a chameleon," I told her.

"I like that idea. Did I tell you my last dream?"

"What's that?

"I was riding on the flatcar of a train. I was naked and had to keep dancing. If I stopped dancing, the whole train would stop and never move again."

We came back outside into the cold, wet Paris night and squeezed into Jean-François' black Porsche. He was still talking excitedly about his project. "What we need today is a private space where people can really get together and celebrate—something to take the place of the lack of rituals, the absence of God. Something like a concrete physical utopia—a place you can go to, stay as long as you like, renew yourself. We'll have Turkish steam rooms, maybe *odalisques*! It'll be a place of repose, of meditation, of sensuality."

Cynthia shook her head. "Sounds good, but I don't think it'll work."

"Why not?"

"Because the truth is always elsewhere."

Jean-François accelerated the black Porsche. Cynthia called it a dark dragon, and so in the speeding dark dragon we soared down the long, shiny Champs-Elysées, lights streaming on both sides. I was just happy to be squeezed next to Cynthia in the back, my hands tight on her long smooth legs.

Midnight in Paris had come. Crowds rushed into holes in the ground, eager for the last metro.

Jean-François cried out, "The old feelings and sensibilities are going to disappear as surely as prehistoric monsters!"

Cynthia urged him on. "Go on, do it, do whatever feels right for you. Create your own utopia!"

Jean-François drove us to Montmartre and we stood on top of the legendary hill overlooking silvery, black-and-white Paris stretched out below us, glittering in half-moonlight. Cynthia's eyes strayed back and forth from the haunted sky to the domed white church, to our own bodies. She started swaying back and forth, dancing in a semi-dream state. "I'm such a bad dancer," she said. "I don't know the music or the words. I only know the feeling and the movement."

Below us Paris plunged down in a black-and-white sea of lights cut by the phantom shapes of the sharply angled slate rooftops.

"Moments don't die," I whispered to Cynthia. I hugged her shoulders. "The best ones just keep repeating themselves forever."

Jean-François had rolled a joint with *Zizi* cigarette paper and was now inhaling the sweet-smelling Moroccan grass.

A humped-over beggar woman passed us carrying two large bags stuffed with red and yellow rags.

Jean-François passed Cynthia the joint and she took a deep toke.

I kissed her passionately on the back of her neck and behind the little lobes of her ears.

"I feel so good," she sighed. "Whatever it is that's going on, I just don't want it to stop."

CHAPTER 34

▼

People were arriving *chez* Jean-François for dinner. In the background played music by the Beatles and Bob Dylan. There was Bobby Kornfeld, a balding American expatriate who had set up a hugely successful overseas mutual fund investment service in Switzerland. There was Judy's cousin, Matt, head of IBM's computer service operations in San Francisco, and Suzanne, a vivacious American anthropologist who worked for UNESCO and was trying to raise funds for a research trip to Africa. Jean-François was proudly showing off a "Marilyn" painting by Andy Warhol he had just purchased from an up-and-coming gallery in New York City.

"Look at that image," he marveled. "That's pretty damn good. I think there's something tragic in it, don't you?"

"Her cheeks are a little too silvery," his wife, Judy, commented.

This angered Jean-François. "Be quiet! What do you know about American painting anyway? Of course her cheeks should be silver. That's the only way they could possibly be!"

"If you look at them carefully, they grow darker on you," Suzanne remarked in her husky voice. "By the way, Jean-François," she added, "when are you going to loan me the money I need to go to Africa and make my film in Niger? That's Niger, not Nigeria. The President invited me to stay in his palace. He even built an indoor skating rink to keep himself cooled off in the sultry hot weather."

That night the Olympic games in Mexico were on TV. While everyone watched, Cynthia glanced through a French edition of *Playboy*.

"Look at these enormous breasts—and then watch the black swimmers. Interesting combination."

"Gee guys," said Judy. "The Americans are winning. That's beautiful, that's great."

"Beautiful! Great!" Jean-François sneered. "Is there anything the Americans have that isn't beautiful and great?"

Three victorious black athletes raised their hands in the clenched fist black power salute.

Cynthia disappeared into the bathroom with Ode.

Titi, the piano player, was telling everyone how when he was in Tunisia he had an operation on his head: his skull had been drilled open between his eyes, to release the pressure, he said, to enable blood to flow more freely, to help activate his "third eye."

"Can you see better?" Judy asked him.

"It only works if first you stand on your head for at least three minutes," Titi answered. "It brings a sudden surge of blood to the front of your forehead. It's the best way of getting and staying high."

Titi sprang to his hands and, in an instant, was standing on his head, his feet propped against the wall.

"Long live ze decadence," laughed Jean-François nasally in English. "Long live ze ugliness."

Suzanne was telling me, "I've really got to get out of Paris—it's so stifling here! Like a fish bowl. Some friends of mine are flying in a few days to Niger in a small plane. I think I'll go with them. I want to do a film on certain magical practices there. In Paris I'm just so bored and sick to death with myself."

"How can you be bored in Paris?" I wondered.

"But what should I do?" she insisted. "In what direction do you think I should go?"

"But do you think there's any 'right' path? Any 'true' direction? As if that existed anywhere outside of ourselves?"

I turned away, but her hand was lying over mine, just gently touching. The compassion I felt for her started to morph into a crude stirring of desire.

Judy went into the kitchen to check on the roast. "You know, Jean-François is just too French! He doesn't give a shit about me or about anyone. He thinks I'm stupid just because I'm an American and I'm not as clever as he is. Sometimes I wonder what I'm doing with him and I have this feeling that I got on the wrong train."

"A train you can always get off," I reminded her.

"But then I'm afraid I'd be left behind at the station."

Cynthia and Ode came back. They were clasping hands and smiling as if they shared an important secret.

Titi was still "standing" upside down, balanced now against a corner of the dining room. His crossed legs and his hieratic, immobile pose made him look like an inverted African sculpture.

We sat down for dinner around a long, heavy, wooden medieval table Jean-François said he had inherited from his family. It came from some thirteenth-century monastery, he said. Monks had once used the bowls that had been hollowed out in its surface for eating soup.

Matt, the computer expert, had flown in that day from Holland on his private jet, along with his wife, a scrawny, thin California woman, her three Yorkshire terriers, and a pretty eighteen-year-old Dutch girl, his "assistant." He related how he was building a new ultra-modern dwelling outside of San Francisco exactly on the epicenter of the San Andreas Fault.

"We're doing a whirlwind tour of Europe," his wife said.

"Yes," Matt went on. "France at a glance. Ten cities in ten days. We'll try anyway. Having your own plane makes it so much easier!"

"When you travel like that, it's probably hard to remember anything," Cynthia remarked.

"Not true!" he snapped back. "I'll never forget that bridge in Provence that Van Gogh built!"

There was an outburst of general laughter, an epic of snorting and sneezing.

I was seated next to Suzanne at the table end. She had her knee pressed firmly against the inside of my leg. Surprised, I stared at her. She met my gaze and smiled.

"All of you will soon see!" I heard Cynthia announcing prophetically. She rose from her chair, as if to make a toast, and, pointing to Matt, declared, "This year is going to hit you with something you never expected! It'll be totally spontaneous and free and have nothing to do with your technology and rationality and efficiency."

The computer expert haruumphed. Jean-François snickered. Judy tried to relieve the tension, "Does anyone want a *crème brûlée* from Chez Fauchon?"

"It's my *crème brûlée!*" Jean-François interrupted her. "I went and bought it! The only thing you own in the kitchen is a bottle of milk!"

Suzanne's leg was now pressed aggressively against my own, her knee yawing up between my thighs. Instead of pushing her away, I found myself putting my hand under the table edge and caressing her fishnet stockings. I sensed a vibration in her, a vital earthy power.

Cynthia's crystalline voice floated plaintively from across the table, "Let's get some fresh air. Let's go outside and take a midnight walk in the Luxembourg gardens."

They all turned their heads and looked at me, expecting a scene. But I had already realized I could not resist the power of the moment. I felt like, *Whatever happens, will happen. If it's pleasant, it will be good. If it's not pleasant, it will pass.*

Then, with a clatter of dancing, flying feet, Cynthia and Ode exited together. Titi, now on his feet, meandered after them, as if drawn by the vortex they left in their wake. I knew the right thing to do was to get up and go after her, but I didn't.

"That American girl, Cynthia," the computer expert commented. "She's beautiful, but so unstable. She smiles, she laughs, she says all these things you don't expect—she's really wonderful."

"*Non, non,*" shrugged Jean-François. "She's just crazy and sex-starved like so many of those American student girls who come to Paris. She needs a good lover. It's so simple, really."

"A French lover, of course," Judy cut in sarcastically.

"But you are right, *mais oui, ma chérie,* of course, of course, only French!"

It was late, and I had drunk too much. When I left I lurched down the stairs descending from the sixth floor three at a time. The timer-device light kept going out. Suzanne was behind me, groping after me in the darkness of the stairwell. I started to laugh, at first softly, then furiously and uproariously, and she asked, "What are you laughing about? What's so funny?"

I didn't know how to tell her, and then she started laughing, and when we were finally in the narrow street leaning against an old wall plastered with ripped posters, she flung her arms around me and I embraced her. In that moment I forgot about Cynthia and everything else and went back to her apartment filled with the magic and strange power of all her African objects.

CHAPTER 35

▼

I did not think that I was committing an infidelity toward Cynthia until the next morning at gray breaking Paris dawn when I again stumbled down four flights of stairs into the street and then knew in my real heart that I had.

They were washing down the sidewalks in front of the cafés on the broad, tree-lined avenues, and unstacking the tables and chairs. There was the sweet bitter smell of espresso and freshly baked croissants. I bought some and brought them back for Cynthia.

I felt a deep, humbling pain. I did not know why I had done what I had done. I had violated the trust of my own desire. There was the nostalgia for a lost honesty, an irrecoverable purity.

Cynthia saw that I was troubled and said, "Look at you, coming back with your tail between your legs! Are you worrying about the way you behaved last night? About what you did? Stupid! Do you want to be with that big Suzanne? Does she interest you? Does she excite you? Then go off and feel free to fuck her!"

I stared at Cynthia, speechless.

"Look," she explained, "We're each free beings, right? It doesn't matter what you do. Haven't you understood that by now? You could go out in the damn street and stand on your head all day just like Titi, it wouldn't matter at all."

"You wouldn't say that if you didn't feel guilty about something yourself," I countered. "You're just trying to redeem yourself by these offers of liberty."

"Of course I feel guilty. That's precisely the problem. We all feel guilty. We are made to feel guilty from the beginning; from the moment we are born there is guilt. It is laid on us—there is guilt about this, guilt about that, we've got to jump out of the circle, derail the train ..."

"It's easy to say we're free beings, but it's hard to act freely without creating pain for someone else."

"But we are free beings," she insisted, looking up at me with tearful shining eyes. "It's the only thing that matters, really. If we love each other, we should be free, not cripple ourselves with our love."

"So you're saying we can do anything we want, follow our wildest desires to the end?"

"Yes, yes, because the only way to free yourself of them, is to live through them and beyond them. You can laugh, cry, dance, sing, shout, weep, shriek, gesticulate—you know life has no meaning other than the living of it. With your talents you ought to be able to go right through it, just do exactly as you please. That's what I'm telling you."

I knew that this freedom Cynthia evoked was part of the "new age morality." It had to do with the violent explosion of sex, music, and drugs that we were beginning to live. Yet what was the cost of it? Where would it lead Cynthia and her friends and myself, I wondered. So I wavered, torn, suddenly aware of obscure disasters waiting to happen. "So we'll just go on as we are," I murmured. "You and me, me and you, here, now, in Paris."

"That's not enough," she declared. "There's more."

She tossed a diaphanous purple shawl around her shoulders and swirled gypsy-style a few steps around me, pretending to pull imaginary flowers out of the air from behind my brooding head.

That night it rained heavily and she woke up panicked and grabbed me and said she had had a nightmare and we had grown very old and the dust of ancient age was settling over our bodies, but neither of us could give up our souls and die peacefully for fear of leaving the other alone.

CHAPTER 36

▼

For a few days we were together again. We stopped seeing other people and spent time in silence and learning again how to inhabit the house of love. On Sunday we went to visit Napoleon's tomb and walked in the cold, clear light along the sweeping esplanade of Les Invalides.

"You know something?" she asked me, hanging on my arm. "It's easy as pie."

"What?"

"Oh, to love. To make your head and your heart vibrate with the same feeling, to know how to dance, to live in the moment, to be alive now."

She circled around me, making soft, alluring gestures with her hands.

"I worry about your feelings for Charlie. I'm worried you might leave me for him."

"But nothing is ze matter, but nothing!" she cried in fake French. We both laughed.

It was Charlie who had told me, "We are all looking for great moments in life but actually it's the special little moments that make up the value and become irreplaceable."

As we swung toward the golden dome under which Napoleon lay buried, I squeezed her hand and felt that aching sensation of living something very rare that could never be repeated.

Later we met Charlie by chance at Le Coupole and had a drink with him. Jean-Paul Sartre and Simone de Beauvoir were seated near us at their favorite corner table.

"How's life, kiddo?" Charlie asked.

"Not bad, not bad—*pas mal, pas mal.*"

"It's better than nothing, kiddo, and every day it's getting better. Everything is possible, no?"

"Emotions are possible," Cynthia said. "Getting out of your head and into your feelings."

"What emotions?"

"Flowers, lights, joy, love ..."

"Ah, c'mon," Charlie muttered. "You make it sound too cute."

"It's only as cute as you want it to be."

She let Charlie hug her and he pecked her French-style on both cheeks. He must have sensed my anxiety. "Tough nuts, kiddo," he said.

It was a relief to guide her through the revolving doors and out onto the boulevard Montparnasse again.

"Tell me one thing," I urged, embracing her. "Say you love me. Say the word, just one word, go on, say it!"

"Quakquak, quakquak, quakquak!" she mocked, twisting herself loose.

"You are really crazy," I said, trying to grab her arms again.

"Go away! No! Go away!"

"No, never. I won't leave you! I won't go away."

I struggled with her, trying to pull her toward me.

She suddenly stopped resisting me, her body became limp. She angled her head, raised her eyebrows and coyly said, "Okay, so you want to play? Then let's go home and play, really play."

"Yes, *oui*," I affirmed. "Let's play the flower game, let's play the love game, let's go back and play together deeply and truly and mean it."

As soon as we stepped into the apartment I started kissing her, my kisses tumbling down the side of her long-stemmed neck. Her hips trembled as she wrapped her legs around me. She balanced on my feet, poised on her toes, her breasts pressed hard against me. I picked her up and laid her on the bed. I blanketed her with my body, trying to erase everything in my mind but the new powerful feeling that was surging between us.

I whispered in her ear, "Cynthia, my Cynthia, my treasure, my sea, my murmur, my ocean, my memory, my wave, my love, my life ..."

My straining body slipped and slid massively into her; she sighed and gasped. It was as if we had been pressed together in an ecstatic union by two huge pounding cylinders. The shell of her sex opened sweetly to receive me. That grand "forever" smile came across her bright face; great, causeless laughter began to trickle between us. How funny we were! How funny everything was! How beautiful and strange life was! How very simple.

"I love you Cynthia," I cried out in my ecstasy.

At last we had truly come together. Was it too late or too early? Was it possible, was it true, would it last? The image of this physical perfection, of this fearful totality and unity, made me cry out again. I wanted to hide my poor face; I felt I had glimpsed "It."

Serenely she embraced me as our bodies, entangled, mirrored each other. My seed was sprinkled over the lower part of her belly. She touched it and called it "magic gunpowder."

This love-making appeased my torn mind and gave me the illusion of a new solidity and continuity. With the stubbornness of a beginner, I kept trying to return to that point where we had first loved each other, from where hopefully we could begin again.

Her simple nudity invariably excited me, but there were times when, in spite of my desire, she seemed not to take it seriously. One night in particular she just kept on laughing. "Whoosh! Whoosh!" she went with her lips, as if the wind were running through her hair. She took a match and lit all the candles she could find. She took my letters and manuscripts and piled them up in front of a makeshift altar.

"This is the altar of memory," she said. "Now let's destroy it." And so it was burned, except for a few notebooks I managed to save which later helped form the content of this book.

CHAPTER 37

▼

There was a demonstration in front of the American Embassy to protest the Vietnam War. It had been organized by Jean-François' magazine *The Underground Sun*. Cynthia, wearing blue jeans and an oversized gray sweater, met me in front of the illuminated, hieroglyphed obelisk on the pace de la Concorde. Shadowy figures darted in and out of the gathering crowds. Fires were lit, flags burned. Flanked by the great lions, we leaned over the stone balustrade of the Tuileries garden and listened to the cries and chants of the students.

A middle-aged man with no legs was pushing himself around frantically in his wheelchair, a huge banner fluttering over his head that proclaimed, "Down with American imperialism, Puritanism, denial of sexuality and of the values of all men!"

Suddenly, with a shrill, intermittent honking, a convoy of big blue police vans began pulling up, and strange, helmeted men that looked as if they were from Mars, streamed out like ants, carrying shields and wielding clubs. There was panic and uproar. Many tried to flee. With a sickening feeling, I heard the sound of wood cracking against bone. People scattered in all directions, stark with fear, while a few angry ones surged forward toward the American Embassy, as if trying to scale the walls. They were chanting, "What about the bombings? How many more? How many more?"

I grabbed Cynthia's hand to keep her from being swept away by the fleeing crowd. The French *flics* were everywhere, it was useless to resist. The demonstration had been announced; there was no element of surprise. Before I knew what was happening, two cops pinned my arms from behind and dragged me into the back of a French police van, known as a "black Maria." Once I was inside, other cops kept kicking me and trying to club me over the head. I was taken to a police station where I spent the night in a filthy jail cell in the company of a small, skinny French youth who kept endlessly repeating the Aznavour song, "And now what am I going to do?" (*Et maintenant que vais-je faire?*).

As soon as I was released, I rushed back to the flat, hoping to find Cynthia. She was already there, she was fine. When she saw me, "Hurry," she said. "Quick. Come inside."

Softly and deftly she helped me undress, she told me to relax, she ran a bath for me and bandaged my bruises. She told me to descend, to enter into her, to find peace in her luminous body again.

But it was difficult for me to find a center, something in me still angrily raging.

"Revolt leads to nothing, you know," she said. "Resisting something just makes you part of what you're resisting. Rebellion creates only confusion and hostile, futile feelings. What do you think we can fix or change anyway?"

She smiled tenderly. "Do you think you're going to make it any better, my little one?"

I didn't know. What I did regret was the excitement that came from the feeling of fury and revolt that had once been an integral part of my spirit. I had been for anarchic joy and love, firmly against the false cultures created by capitalism, socialism, and communism. In my heart there had always been hope that, even taking into account the Vietnam debacle, better things would prevail.

"We have the resources inside ourselves," Cynthia was telling me. "Everything we need, we already have—it's in our heads, our consciousness, part of our inner kingdom. The potential for utopia is there, but we were just looking for it in the wrong place, on the outside, where the real place to find it is within us, on the inside."

I shook my head. "I don't know," I said. "I don't know quite how one can find a path into that 'inner kingdom.'"

"It's the artists, the poets, musicians and dancers, who will lead us there, the men gifted with imagination, the great wild ones who will make everything blossom! Just think of it: we have no limits ... our love knows no bounds. The secret truths, long-hidden, are rising to the surface. We just have to seize them, make them part of our bodies, of what we are."

"But how do we do that?" I wondered.

"It's easy. We have to work on our heads, because it all comes from the mind. We need to open our minds and to do that we need a tool, and that tool can be grass or hashish or LSD. It's like putting a new magic molecule into your bloodstream and it just circulates round and round, and every now and then it bonks you when you're not aware, and you say, O, man, wow, is it really like that? Can it be as beautiful as that?"

But the freedom I was looking for—had come to Paris to find—had little to do with what Cynthia was now telling me. I felt she had raised the stakes and crossed into a different dimension.

"I'm going out for a while," I said. "I need some time by myself."

Eventually I found myself on the rue Delambre. I joked with the prostitutes on the corner (a mother and daughter team) and wandered into the Rosebud bar. It was 3 AM but the bar was still packed. I found Charlie seated on a stool.

"*Ça va*, big guy?" Charlie asked me. "No good, I can see."

"Cynthia is crazy. I don't know if I can follow her in the direction she wants to go."

"Don't worry about it. With a woman like that, you can't win. I love her too, but she's going to do what she wants to do. Don't let yourself be pulled along in her wake. She can destroy you."

"And you, Charlie?"

"Me, I'm old. Yeah, I'm an old guy and I drink a little bit. I don't know too much, but I know a little, and I also know how to drink a little."

I told him about the anti-war demonstration in front of the U.S. Embassy, how quickly the cops had showed up, how brutal they had been, how I had spent the night in jail.

"*Oui*, yeah, the *flics* are always in control—not just in France, but everywhere. You can't fight tanks with peashooters. Guess what: the fat people always eat the thin people. But if by miracle the thin people ever got fatter than the fat people, then they would eat the fat people too. What else is new?"

Cynthia's words echoed in my head: "Don't try so hard. Just let things be."

Charlie must have been thinking about her too, because he muttered, "Well, kiddo, if you love her, you can have her. You can have her because you love her and deserve her. You don't always get what you deserve, but you can have her if you love her. But I just want you to know that I love her too."

A sudden dark jealousy rose in me. "Enough drinking," I said. "I'm going back now."

"Look, pal, if you want her, you've got to take the good with the bad, it's a package," Charlie called after me.

At the news kiosk on the corner of the boulevard Montparnasse, I stopped to buy that morning's *Herald-Tribune*. A short article said that a small private plane carrying six passengers, including Suzanne, the American anthropologist working for UNESCO, had crashed in dense fog into a mountainside on the Canary Islands. It was on its way to Niger. There were no survivors.

CHAPTER 38

▼

Heavy, lead-colored clouds hung over the great serpentine river. Even the towers of Notre-Dame looked foreshortened by the damp soiled gray light. The excitement of the students continued to spread, but there was no place for it to go. Police vans were on every corner. The nights were cool and hollow like empty drums. Down the wide, well-groomed boulevards the Paris traffic swished ceaselessly.

Ode was again a frequent visitor to our flat. She had let her hair grow back, it was similar to a crew-cut, and it gave her a boyish, almost androgynous look.

"We have to turn toward the East," she announced. "The answer cannot be found in the West. It's certainly not in Paris."

"Right," Cynthia agreed. "I can't take Paris anymore. I need something clear and bright and bigger and different. I feel like I'm stuck in a time warp here that's about to explode."

In the evening, the same moon rose and floated over the ancient Paris rooftops.

I thought more and more about returning to the States. I realized I really didn't care that much about what was happening in the streets of Paris. It was enough to hear it vaguely in the distance like the roaring of the sea.

"It's true," Ode said. "Outside the weather's always bad. I miss my country, the beautiful light of Morocco. We must find a way to go there."

I couldn't free myself of the precarious feeling that everything was just hanging together by a thread, could collapse at any moment. No doubt it was a mistake to have sought safety in the strength of a physical union with this elusive woman. She continued to make some money doing her photo shoots. She would come back exhausted at the end of the day and take a nap. Tense and anxious, growling with discontent, I would circle around her. Sometimes her sensuous immobility would excite me so much that I would try to possess her in her sleep.

One evening, after a long day of work, she reclined peacefully, unaware of my movements. I sought to slip into her before she was fully aware of what was happening.

Startled, she awoke, but she didn't seem upset. She caressed the back of my shoulders and said, "If you want to be one with me, let me show you how."

Later we talked, and she told me, "I know you agree with me because your passion isn't just for me. It's for that greater something beyond me that we're both looking for. I'm looking for clarity and harmony and that bright burning moment of consciousness when you walk through the 'doors of perception.'"

"But tell me, what really do you want?"

"I know what it is," she said, "but I can't tell you what it is. And I don't know if you're going to be able to follow me."

CHAPTER 39

▼

Charlie was having a big *vernissage*, an opening, at the *très chic* Cazenave gallery on the boulevard Saint-Germain. The lush color catalog had an article in it by a well-known critic that compared Charlie's portraits of nude women seated on chairs to the rigor of Giacometti and to the sensuality of later Matisse. Judy and Jean-François were there, as well as Barbara, the American poetess with her investment banker husband, who had flown in from London. Cynthia had invited Ode, who had brought with her a new friend, Dominique de Montagu, whose family owned a significant interest in one of France's major oil-drilling companies. It was said that Dominique, a full-figured but attractive young woman who must have been in her early twenties, had already come into a considerable fortune due to the premature death of some other family member. She had flaming red hair that flowed in thick tresses down her back. She was known for her wit and wildness, a certain late-night partying ability, and her, at times, reckless generosity.

Her companion, ramrod slim, with a mane of sleek black hair, was the Italian "new-wave" film-maker, Fausto Arditi. Champagne was served—Veuve Cliquot—and Cynthia appeared in a lacy, shimmery 1920s style gown. She lit a Winston and vamped playfully in front of one of the many portraits Charlie had done of her.

I could see that Fausto Arditi couldn't take his eyes off of her.

"Do you think you could get me a Johnnie Walker Black Label and water with only a few ice cubes?" Charlie was asking one of the girls serving champagne.

Then Charlie turned to me. "Hey, kiddo, I guess you and I are rivals, no?"

I looked at him and didn't answer.

"I mean, you must know I've been calling Cynthia. I wanted to take her last weekend to see Chartres—you know, the cathedral—early in the morning when the light is just coming up on it over the flat countryside, as Proust described it—you know Proust, right?"

"Look," I said angrily. "You've been in Paris a long time, Charlie. You know what's going on. If you want to take Cynthia out and screw her, go ahead, but just don't ask for my help!"

Charlie mumbled something nervously, the tiny ice cubes shaking in his glass. "Please don't say that to me," he said. "I may be an old man, but I'm not a black dog."

A waiter was passing hors-d'oeuvres made up of pyramids of tomatoes hollowed out and garnished with slivers of egg yoke and caviar. Cynthia clapped her hands and spun once around.

"See, it's a tomato dance."

"*Oui, oui*, to mate her, to mate her!" someone lamely joked.

"What a funny thing a tomato is: it has a red toe."

Everyone laughed. The gallery was filling up with more and more people. You could hardly see the paintings any more.

"Let's get some fresh air," I suggested.

Cynthia and I stepped out onto the Boulevard Saint-Germain. Ode followed us.

"Let me introduce you to Fausto Arditi. You must have seen his last film, about the life of Arthur Rimbaud, how he travels to Ethiopia to find out what his last days were like."

"And this is Dominique de Montagu. She's the producer who helped Fausto make all of his films."

Dominique immediately launched into a complicated story about a wild party she had been to the night before—there had been a mad countess who ran around drinking from everybody's glasses—and how she had left early because she did not want to deal with the debauchery she knew was inevitable at the end of such an evening.

Inside the gallery, Jean-François could be heard vigorously arguing, "But the struggle is long. We must understand that it takes a long time to prepare the masses so that they're ideologically capable of accepting a concrete transformation in the structure of—"

"That's all such bullshit!" Barbara retored. "As if you can change the way people think. Myself, I just want to live."

I wasn't listening so much as watching Cynthia, who now was locked in an intense conversation with Fausto Arditi. He looked different than the photos I had seen of him, his bearded face somehow more haggard and worn. He said he had just come back from doing some film in South America, where he was constantly mistaken for Che Guevara. "Miserable me. I had to keep telling them, I am not who you are think I am, I am someone else!"

A pretty French girl looked curiously at Charlie and asked him, "Tell me, are you an American sometimes?"

"No, I'm an American all the time."

"My father called me today from Casablanca," Ode was saying. "I haven't talked to him since I was a kid. He wanted to know if I could get him a cheap ticket to go to the States. Imagine! After fifteen years! Then he said to me, 'And when are you going to get married?' 'Get married?' I said. What an idea! Don't you think my family poisoned me enough when I was younger?" Ode choked with bitter laughter.

"I was poisoned too," Cynthia said. "My mother was raised until the age of twenty-one in a Catholic convent. All I dreamt of when I was a little girl was getting away, escaping to Paris, becoming a model, a ballet dancer, a flute-player, anything but what I was ..."

"My family is very well-known in France," Dominique de Montagu chimed in. "We go back to the fourteenth century and the first kings of France. They're very upset with me because I don't want to work in their oil business and I don't want to have a husband and a place of my own. A place of my own, *merde*! Shit! The Montagu family just can't imagine what I'm doing—no husband, no home, no job, no path going into the future."

"A lot of people have spent a lot of time trying to advise me," Cynthia concluded. "How I detest it! They're incapable of finding any solution to life for themselves, but think they can tell me how to live. Everything's so fixed and rigid with them."

Charlie came over and started talking about his work. The show had clearly been a big success; red dots indicating "sold" had sprung up as if by magic next to nearly all the paintings.

"I always try to remember the positions and movements of people, so that then I can draw and sketch that movement."

"All work is good at the moment you're doing it," Cynthia countered gaily. "After that, what counts?"

Charlie hesitated, grabbed his drink. "So the moment it's done, it's no longer good? But what's the result, what's delivered?"

Dominique de Montagu smiled; Fausto Arditi was listening too.

"But it shouldn't matter," Cynthia went on. "Everything's going to be swept away anyway. What are you always trying to capture things for? In the end there's nothing but loss."

"Of course, of course. But think of Cézanne or Matisse. How, after months and months, or years, there suddenly comes a painting that gives meaning to all that you've lived."

"Then what are you afraid of? Just do your thing, that's all that counts, baby. But you see, you're stuck in the second and third dimension, you're hung up on space and representation. I'm trying to pass from the first to the fourth."

"What about the fifth?" Dominique de Montagu questioned. "And the sixth, seventh, and infinity? Once I start, I can't stop."

"Neither can I," said Charlie, staring fixedly at her.

Sparkling with her radiant energy, Cynthia surged up in the middle of the gallery; she pretended she had a flute in her hands, as her fingers flew and made imaginary music. She seemed to throw off an aura, an ethereal light.

Charlie could not tear himself away from her. Half-jokingly, he murmured in her ear, "If you weren't young enough to be my granddaughter, I do believe I'd ask you to marry me."

CHAPTER 40

▼

Snow covered the noses of the gargoyles on Notre-Dame. Cynthia slept late. "Too much beautiful food and wine," she murmured.

When I tried to touch her, she groaned, "Oh, don't disturb me." She slumbered amid the thick gray gloom of the late morning. After the events of the night before at Charlie's *vernissage* I felt a need to possess, to reclaim her.

But when I sought to caress her again, she whispered faintly, "Don't touch me when I'm asleep, my body's so heavy."

I lay and leaned above her, grazing my cheek against her own. "Be with me, my love, *mon amour*, Cynthia," I entreated her.

She responded with a sweet moan that encouraged me. From far away in drowsy land she smiled, hinting at vague pleasure. Her pale smooth face was turned away from me. I ran the tips of my fingers around the inside of her turned-up nose.

"Leave me alone, leave me alone," she begged me.

I walked outside up the boulevard Raspail and had an espresso at Le Dome and bought the *Herald-Tribune* at the corner kiosk.

When I came back, I found Cynthia engaged in an animated conversation on the phone. It was with Charlie. The feeling in my heart dropped.

"What are you talking to him for?"

"I'm so sorry," she cried out, like a wounded animal. "But I have to go to him. It's stronger than I am. I felt this thing last night when I was talking to him—it was so strong, so incredibly powerful, wow!"

"But what do you possibly see in him? He himself told you he's old enough to be your grandfather. Why would you leave me for him?"

"I don't know if I'm leaving you. That's just it. I'm like a migratory bird—I need my freedom to fly. But I will come back. Look, let me try to explain it: there's something in Charlie, some wisdom, some toughness, that really attracts me. I have to try."

"But where are you going with him?"

"I don't know yet. He mentioned something about Chartres."

I was dumbfounded. I knew instinctively I could not stop her from going to Charlie. But how could I get close to the inner core, to the impenetrable essence of Cynthia? I had to try something.

So I unbuttoned my pants, took off my pants and socks. Naked I stood in front of her in the half-winter darkness. I stabbed after her as if after a ghost, a distant China sea.

"Just what are you trying to do?" she puzzled. "Rape me?"

"Cynthia, I feel if we could just make love again, in the same way that we used to, everything would be ok."

"Oh, my dear you!" she lamented. "Oh, you! What a fool you are! Don't you know that I do love you? But I can't be with you because it wouldn't work. I live in nature and you live in words in some other space of your mind. All I want to do is be natural and live in nature and have a simple relationship. Charlie told me when life is very beautiful, it is always very simple. Truth is simplicity, truth is beauty, no?"

She threw her arms around me and hugged me with a cool but passionate intensity.

"Let me go to him! I will come back to you, I promise."

I looked at her, some emotion of fury and pain blazing inside me.

"Go ahead," I said. "Do what you have to do. Sleep with him. Fuck him for all I care. And one more thing—don't bother to come back!"

"Oh, my God!" Cynthia wailed. "Let's be free. Let's not kill each other with words, which you don't mean anyway. That's what makes me so sad, you're always trying to separate me from things rather than letting me come in contact with what would make me whole."

"Just go ahead. Do whatever you want. I couldn't care less."

"Please hug me," Cynthia said. "Please. *S'il te plait.* I beg you."

I stood there looking at her blankly. I did not touch her.

I learned later that Charlie took Cynthia with him to visit Chartres Cathedral. Cynthia confided to Judy, who in turn told me, that she had this naïve and crazy idea that Charlie, because of his age and experience, would be able to help her connect.

"He fits my fantasy of an older man who is strong and experienced and willing to master me, someone who will accept me on no other terms but those of a love slave."

"Of course," said Judy, "she must have known in her heart that this experience of being Charlie's 'love-slave' could not go very far, but still, she wanted to live it."

When Cynthia came back a few days later, she was bitterly disappointed because Charlie had turned out to be "all talk and no action." They had stayed in a small hotel in the shadow of the great cathedral, but he had booked two rooms for them. And apparently it was more important for Charlie to drink and eat and talk with Cynthia than to actually make love. "So," Cynthia said, "nothing happened. It was just awful."

I almost felt badly for her.

"Let's talk and try to work it out between us," she suggested. "It's so stupid not to reconcile."

"Okay," I said. "Let's try."

"But first," she smiled, "I want to take you to this fabulous party that Dominique de Montagu is giving tonight."

Cynthia had disappeared with Charlie for a total of three days. Three days for her always marked an important segment of time. I knew it was the limit point beyond which she agreed with Ode that physical love between a man and a woman became hopelessly compromised.

Strangely, I did not feel angry with Charlie. I knew that he was doing what he felt he had to do. He was participating in a wild rush of feeling for a crazy young woman who was too busy living to worry about the endings of what she chose.

Charlie had started his adventure by taking Cynthia to the Louvre, where he showed her his favorite painting, the seated Egyptian scribe. "Look at those eyes, they have an eternal presence," he commented to her.

"Eternal, maternal," Cynthia had mocked him. "I'm hungry."

He had taken her to lunch at Le Coupole where they nibbled on *crevettes grises*, which Cynthia called ocean peanuts, and Charlie drank a Carlsberg beer and a half-bottle of Brouilly.

Lunch arrived. It was *poule au pot*, chicken in the pot, with a white wine sauce. After they had finished, Charlie held it up and said, "Would you like the carcass?"

"Yes, yes."

"How about the liver of the chicken. Do you want that?" He held it up, dark and shiny.

"I do," Cynthia said.

"And the chicken heart?"

"I want the soul!" Cynthia teased him.

"Sorry," replied Charlie. "I just ate it, raw!"

Charlie smoked his Lucky Strikes, the ice cubes clinked in his Black Label and soda, and later he took Cynthia back to his studio and asked her if she would pose for him. She removed her clothes and stretched out, odalisque-like, on his monastic bed.

"Draw me like this," she said.

But Charlie said he couldn't, because the sensuality of her reclining nude posture conflicted with the visual reality of her he had in his head. So he had her sit on a chair and he painted only her torso. In his portrait her hair was shorn and she had large stark eyes.

Cynthia broke the silence. "Make love to me. I want you to make love to me now Charlie."

He approached her, stood behind her, rested his creased hands on her bare shoulders.

"I want to but I can't," he said simply. "I drink too much, it's no good. And I like you and want to be with you, but I don't care that much about sex. No, I guess I like the blue and gray light here in my studio. And, you know, sometimes what makes me the happiest is just being able to go out and cross the street."

Yet Cynthia stayed with him for another night, hoping that she could make him change his mind and that he would yield to her.

On Saturday they had lunch at Chez Flo in Montmartre, where they had oysters and langoustines with mayonnaise and drank cool Sancerre. Afterwards they strolled around the place du Tertre, and Charlie said, "You know, Cynthia, when I was trying to make a living after the war, I thought I could make some money by coming up here and painting those lousy crap imitation Utrillos they sell to the tourists, but I couldn't do it, I was a failure."

And you can't make love to me either, Cynthia thought.

She could not forgive him for that, and on the third night she left him and returned to me.

CHAPTER 41

▼

"Hello you! Look at the bright red tulips I brought you, and wake up!"

That was the note I found on my bed the next morning. Cynthia was not there. She must have risen early. I went out looking for her on the terraces of the cafés around Montparnasse. I didn't find her either at Le Dome or at Le Coupole. She was across the street at Le Select, seated at the third row of tables in the corner.

She smiled when she saw me but said nothing. She kept writing with a Bic pen on a black-and-white school notebook. I sat next to her, ordered a *petit-crème*, and watched her write. She didn't seem to mind that I read what she was writing:

> *Monday morning. To wake up and know the day is yours—or mine, for I am only speaking of myself now. Ouf! I am so tired of men, of all their ideas and convictions, of how much they drink and of how little they actually do! I just cannot deal with it any more.*
>
> *Charlie was the straw that broke this little camel's back. He wanted too much and gave me so little, and he couldn't give me what I wanted. Why is it that in myself I feel such a sensation of breadth and great expansiveness? Now this whole day stretches before me and it is mine to live, and all I can do is sit here in this dumb French café and write about it—poorly, even unwillingly, I admit, since it is against my desire just to live. Writing about this day will not enable me to live it any better. Yet words, too, come from a human being. I feel like an adolescent again, wondering about these things.*
>
> *It's good to be alone, I need solitude and space. I don't want any men or any demands upon me and I don't want to have to fulfill the banal requests of anyone else ...*

What a thrilling sensation, to be alone, after having spent three days trying to figure out another person, bending myself to his will and desire. I don't want to have to say bonjour *and look* jolie; *I don't want anyone pawing at my thighs. Ah, to live and breathe in Paris,* vivre et respirer à Paris, *that's all I want. It's a little but it's a lot (*c'est peu mais c'est tout*) …*

"I'm sure you agree, *n'est-ce pas?*" she said in a tone that was slightly defiant. Stunned, I sat looking at her.

"Oh, I know what you're thinking. We're all caught in such webs of sentimentalism and fear to move in new interesting directions, that when something does present itself, we don't know what to do."

The keen, biting pain of what she had written rushed through me and told me that this was, indeed, life—I was really living it, and something had to be done, but what?

Just then Ode appeared, with a dark, curly-haired, three-year-old boy in tow. "This is my son, Jemal," she said. "Isn't he beautiful? He's going to be a prince of the desert when he grows up."

"I had no idea you had a son!" I exclaimed.

"Yes, three years ago, in Casablanca. His father's a very powerful man, a close friend of the king, and he only agrees to send my son to Paris to see me once a year for a few days."

"Only once a year? That's nothing."

"Yes, he takes care of him, but he only lets me see him once a year. In a Moroccan court, I would never win, so I have to accept."

"It's such a little time, no?" said Cynthia.

"Yes, it's very little, but think about it: how many days a year do you need to feel truly happy? If I'm truly happy even for one day, that's enough for me. And I'm happy today, because Jemal is with me."

Looking at Cynthia, she added, "But you are sad, *triste*, my dear. That's not the way to be."

"She's unhappy because she ran away with Charlie and it didn't work out," I said.

"That's nothing," Ode replied. "Don't even think about it. It's just one cloud on the surface of the beautiful sky. You know, Cynthia's the most transparent girl I've ever met, she's so clear you can see for miles right down into her."

"Yeah, right," I thought. "You can see so far down into her that what you see nearly blinds you."

I left fifty francs on the zinc tabletop for the bill, bought a pack of Marlboros, grabbed Cynthia by the arm and walked back with her to our flat near the Montparnasse cemetery.

I sensed that a defining moment was about to erupt between us. If she had had an affair with Charlie, I could forgive her for that, in the same way that she had chosen to overlook the one night I had spent with Suzanne. We were even, and what I wanted was to have the chance to touch her wild elusive body again, to caress her forgivingly, to enter into her deep peace and luminous softness.

I remembered the first morning I had awoken with her and she had whispered, "Bonjour, my big lion, wipe the sleep dust from your eyes and come into my arms." Now I was worried that, if I did not lose her to Charlie, I might lose her to someone or something else.

She had locked herself in the bathroom. I pounded at the door. "Get away!" she shouted. "Beat it! Just leave me alone."

I had tried my best with Cynthia. It was hard to believe that, once again, she was refusing me.

"Please come out, Cynthia," I entreated. "I just want to talk to you."

"Enough talk, you're always talking, you're a walking talk-man. Just leave me alone, that's all I want."

"I'll leave you alone, I promise. Just let's try one last time to be wild and free and true together."

"No, no," she insisted. "I cannot be confined any more. I cannot be made to be the slave of anyone else's desires. It's all so stupid and brutal!"

"Okay, have it your way," I said. "I'm leaving."

CHAPTER 42

▼

Charlie had agreed to meet me at the Rosebud bar on rue Delambre. I needed to know what had actually transpired with Cynthia that weekend, what had made her so angry.

Charlie was sitting at the bar with his usual Black Label and soda in front of him. His rough hands shook slightly as he jingled the two or three ice cubes.

"I always lived as if I were throwing the dice," he muttered in a somber tone. "I did it with Cynthia. Sorry, pal."

"Sorry doesn't cut it, Charlie. You shouldn't have taken her away with you. You shouldn't have done it."

"I guess I'm just not the right guy for her. Somewhere out there there's a right guy, but it's not this one."

"But what did you do with her?" I asked. "How did you manage to hurt her so much?"

Charlie did not answer at once. He shook his head. "It's no use, pal. I'm going to go back to my paintings, to my work. I'll create a homage to Cynthia that will be incredible. I see it now: she'll be emerging out of the distance, like a vision, like a woman on a mountain, or maybe astride a horse … or even sitting on a chair, I don't know …"

"Charlie, I thought you were my friend. I just can't forgive you for this."

"Do you want me to go out and buy a gun? You can use it to shoot me."

"No, Charlie, what I want is much simpler: I want you to apologize to her for hurting her as much as you have."

"I can't do that, pal. Life's life. *La vie c'est la vie*. What is, is. What was, was. I can't make it go away by saying I'm sorry."

A sudden rage came over me, and before I knew what I was doing, I hit Charlie's chin at an angle. Surprised, he fell back, but managed to avoid slipping off the barstool. He was still grasping his drink.

All right, pal. If that's the way you want it."

"It is," I said and walked out.

When later I related this incident to Cynthia, it upset her even more. "You fool! You idot!" she attacked. "You're so damn possessive, you're killing us. Whatever hope there was for us as a couple, you just destroyed it. Don't you realize there was never anything between Charlie and myself, absolutely nothing!"

"Like the fact you went to Chartres with him is all in my imagination."

"Can't we just forget about it?" she asked.

A few nights later Charlie called and invited us both to a Russian restaurant, Chez Natasha, and we enjoyed caviar and *blinis* and *Stolichnaya*, and we laughed and joked as if we were all the best of friends.

CHAPTER 43

▼

"It's curious, even if I knew that something I was doing was dangerous, capable of leading to my death or absence, I doubt if I'd stop doing it ... I'm quite sure I would not ..." Cynthia's voice trailed off. Squatting on her fine sleek haunches, she turned to me, "We know each other now, don't we? We help each other. We're having a good time in Paris. Everything's hunky-dory."

"What?" After all that had happened, I could only wonder what she really meant.

"Hunky-dory," she repeated the phrase with a sort of finality.

I lay and watched her across the subtle white distance of the bed sheets.

"There's that party Dominique de Montagu's giving tonight, remember," she said.

"I don't care about going. Parties bore and exasperate me."

Impulsively I started kissing her, her neck, her fluid shoulders. I felt a need to control, to dominate her. Pressing her to me, I rocked my hips back and forth.

"You're so funny," she laughed. "Your antics amuse me. Hey, you know what I'm going to do? I'm going to fix your big thing, your *truc*.

At first I thought she was going to lift my straining sex into her hands and appease me. But she surprised me, saying, "Come, follow me."

Leaping over the scattered cushions, she tugged me upstairs into the tiny bathroom. She opened the medicine cabinet and drew forth a bottle of sleeping pills. Then she lifted up my penis and, cradling the vibrant purple head in the hollow of her hands, she pretended to open the "mouth" of my penis, to feed my sex a sleeping pill.

"There, this will make your rose *truc* all better," she smiled quickly, laughing.

"You're so damn crazy, silly, just like a child. Come on, we're late, let's go to Dominque's *fête*."

Dominique de Montagu's parties were famous. She was wealthy and she knew it and she liked to make people "feel the scent of her money." She also prided herself on being super hip and liked to think she was capable of the most outrageous gestures. She wore expensive jewelry and flaunted her flaming red hair. The party, given in her family's old palace in Paris' exclusive 7th arrondissement, was already in full swing when Cynthia and I arrived.

Vera, the new "hot" Russian model was there, together with Fausto Arditi, the celebrity Italian film-maker. I said hello to Ode, always surprised to see how she had cropped all her hair. I noticed Titi, the jazz musician, already standing on his head in one corner of a room, while someone else tried to explain to Dominique how the constant blood rush to the front of his forehead helped him to maintain the opening of his "third eye."

Judy was trying to convince a Greek diplomat, supposedly a close friend of Onassis, that he should help them by investing seed money in her husband's "dynamic living center."

Dominique introduced us to a famous poet from San Francisco who was on his way to Cambodia. He was a rough-looking, hard-cut, bearded man with a strangely soft, almost feminine voice that failed to match his appearance. "You can't judge this poet's book by his cover," Dominique joked.

Some French aristocrats, who had attended an evening at the opera, circled around observing everything in their black tie costumes.

The *fête* was being held in honor of the San Francisco poet, and everyone said they were happy to see him because he represented a free, explosive, revolutionary life that, for the most part, was unavailable to them.

When the poet said he was stopping in Rome to "protest something," Dominique asked him, "But what happens if they don't listen to you or give you what you want?"

"I'll just tell them Jackie Kennedy is fucking the Pope!" he replied.

Dominique pretended to be astonished.

"'Fuck'—do you know exactly what that means?" the San Francisco poet insisted.

She shook her head and pointed at me, as if expecting me to provide a precise definition.

Cynthia came up and took Dominique de Montagu aside and whispered its meaning in her ear.

Ode added, "Did you know that in the Arabic language, the word *fuq* also means to go above, to transcend?"

"Oh," exclaimed Dominique. "It's the same as getting high, no?"

On a wine-dark red leather sofa near the great fireplace, a couple had already shed most of their clothes and, with earnest intensity, were swaying in a kind of vibratory snake dance.

"Wow, look at that couple couple!" said the San Francisco poet. Scornfully he added, "I know the girl, she's a real bitch."

Dominique was still standing next to us and I could feel her nerves throbbing with an unbearable tension, as if she were participating in the act herself.

Everyone now stood watching in quasi-religious awe as the young man and woman reciprocated in and out of each other, soundlessly, efficiently as well-oiled machines.

"How awful!" said Ode. "There's not even a spark of passion or joy."

"Hey, I don't believe it, they're actually banging each other!" exclaimed Judy, unable to believe her eyes.

Jean-François, her husband, sneered, "They do that and they think they're alive! What a joke!"

"*Excusez-moi*, Jean-François believes too much in Descartes to accept that. He thinks a man has to think in order to be."

Cynthia was talking with Fausto Arditi when Dominique approached her and said, "I feel so wonderful tonight, everyone is expressing themselves with … such freedom, ah!" She put her arm around Cynthia. "Most people are deaf, you know—deaf! You just can't say anything to them. But you, dear girl, I've always had a special feeling for you, a sense that you have a gift for life and can express yourself directly and spontaneously."

"*Si, si*, you are so right!" Fausto Arditi broke in. "Before I came here tonight I had no idea what I was going to do for my next film, but now I can see and feel it so clearly!"

Dominique, showing more and more excitement, her red tresses blazing, embraced both of them. "I also have an idea," she said. "Listen everyone!" she tapped her glass as if making a toast. The others stopped talking while she spoke. "I had not planned this, but now I realize this is absolutely the right time. So this is what I offer: I will give ten thousand dollars in cash to anyone here who has an original idea or project that in some way contributes to the advance of civilization. You must be willing to act out your idea and to document it on film."

"But what kind of a project, Dominique?" someone asked.

"Anything you like, as long as it involves travel outside of France, that you document it with film, and that in some way it relates to my idea of showing the death of the old ways of being and seeing and feeling, and, of course, the birth of the new ways, which you know."

"When can we start?"

"Tomorrow I will have a cashier's check made out for ten thousand dollars. Anyone who is interested, just come see me, describe your project, and, if I like it, I will give you the money, no problem, no strings. This is my investment in the future!"

"Wow, that's a really great offer, Dominique! You are so generous." Cynthia embraced her warmly on both cheeks.

Dominique smiled, feeling euphoric, flush with the success of her extravagant gesture. Her long mane of reddish hair shone lustrous and fine in the light. On the wine-dark red couch the young couple resumed their relentless rhythm. Others were rolling joints, and Ode produced a shining silver Moroccan water-cooled hashish pipe.

"I have a marvelous idea for a project," she said. "You could go to the south of France, where they make the wine, and you could do a film that would celebrate the burning of the grape."

"Why not go further? What about Athens? Wouldn't it be fantastic to have a film showing me on the Acropolis symbolically burning the vine, because civilization began in Athens, right?"

"Yes, and then you could stop in Cairo and make a pilgrimage to the pyramids and do something to celebrate love and freedom."

"Yes, that would be extraordinary, a real, liberating gesture," Dominique de Montagu approved.

On the way home Cynthia was very excited, leaping up and gamboling a few steps on every sidewalk bench. As soon as we past the door, she tumbled on me and laughed and said, "I want to turn you over and make you lose control, you big, gloomy lion!"

"Don't leave me now. I don't want you running off to some exotic destination just because that crazy Dominique may give you $10,000."

"But, don't you see? It's fate! I must go! I need to get into some other reality that's not based on logic and numbers, and it won't be longer than twenty-one days, I promise."

"Why twenty-one days?"

"Because that's the magic number—three days for a man and twenty-one days for a trip."

Her "project," as she explained to Dominique, and I found out later, was to leave Paris and travel around the world on a sort of reverse pilgrimage, starting in Athens, the cradle of Western civilization, and ending up in the northern Arizona desert near Sedona. She would be the "star" in this film about the beginning and end of Western culture. Dominique loved the idea, and a few days later provided her with the fifty thousand francs necessary to implement it.

CHAPTER 44

▼

Immediately upon waking, I was aware of a terrible absence: Cynthia was gone. There was no note, no sign. Her absence was complete. Total silence reigned in the heavy air of the dark studio. I felt an aching wound in my heart. I understood now how much I had loved her; what I did not understand was how I had lost her. I had come to Paris looking for something, and I had found it. It was a quest for real life, for that "eternal ephemeral" which Cynthia had embodied. For a while I sat as if paralyzed in the wicker chair next to her closet still crammed full with her home-made, Matisse-style clothing. Then the phone rang. It was Charlie.

"Cynthia's gone," I blurted out, still stunned. "Can you imagine, she left without a note, without a word, nothing!

"I know," said Charlie. "I know where she is. I'll tell you about it. Meet me at the Closerie des Lilas in half an hour."

At the back of the café, in a bubbling glass tank, large lobsters were trying to claw their way slowly toward a freedom that never would be theirs. Charlie's expression was tight, somber. He had the grim air of a man who has suddenly come into contact with a violent reality.

"She called me just before she left," Charlie said. "She wanted me to tell you. She couldn't do it herself. She's gone off with that friend of Dominique's, that Italian film-maker, Fausto Arditi."

"Fausto? No, I don't believe it."

"Yes, it happened suddenly. Dominque was just handing out money for her special projects, Fausto had the camera and equipment, so they just went to the airport and caught the early morning Air France flight to Athens."

"But what for?" I wondered. "What could they possibly be going to do?"

"I don't know, pal. You'd have to talk to her friend, Ode. I know they had some idea about going back to the roots of civilization."

The *garçon* brought a pack of Lucky Strikes and two espressos to the table.

"Listen, kiddo," Charlie went on, "I was really in love with her. It was serious between us. I'll never forget that night in Chartres, the hotel room next to the cathedral—the way she kept looking out the window and wouldn't let me touch her, and then when I tried to touch her—"

"I loved her too," I said sadly. "I just realized it now. Too late."

"Better late than never."

"She was angry with me because I'd get jealous of all her relationships. You know how in demand she was. Well, she was always telling me, 'Don't be so possessive, we're all tearing at each other, we say life is beautiful and we're doing the best we can do destroy it. Let me be, let me do what I have to do,' that's what she said over and over again, like a prayer."

"Yeah," admitted Charlie. "She was right, you know. You and I both fell into the old man-woman trap."

"I'm just sorry about what happened between you and me, Charlie."

"We used to be friends," he answered. "I believe we still can be. But I have to tell you, I do love Cynthia, and if she came back, I'd do everything I damn well could to be with her."

"This isn't a game," I said angrily.

"Yes, okay, I know. But I think a great deal of her. If it's necessary, I'm ready to burn all my paintings. You think I cling to them? I don't. When in doubt, choose life, always!"

"Somehow I don't believe you, Charlie. Anyway, she's not here, and she can't help either of us now."

He lit a Lucky. "We're all nervous. It's like a big family—we're nervous, we don't know what to do with each other, we feel perhaps we ought to do something."

"I came to Paris to get away from all that family stuff and now I find myself right smack in the middle of it again."

"It's my fault, pal," Charlie said. "I started it. I'm old enough to be her grandfather, for Christ's sake. What a mistake to start messing around with her!"

"It doesn't matter," I said, getting up to go. "It really doesn't matter any more at all."

A few nights later, well after midnight, I received a collect call from Athens.

"Where are you? What are you doing?"

"I'm okay. I'm in Athens with Fausto. Tomorrow he's going to film at the Acropolis. I'll be wearing all white. We're going to light a big fire and symbolically burn the vine."

"What nonsense!" I shouted. "What's the point?"

"I don't think so. I'm so tired of you and Charlie and all your male friends telling me what to do. I'm here with Fausto and we're having a great time. In a few days we're going to Cairo to film the pyramids, and then to Istanbul for the Blue Mosque, then to Indonesia and Borobodur, and Japan and the temples in Kyoto, and finally to Arizona, where we'll meet in the desert with some holy Indians and begin the cycle again."

"That's completely crazy!" I bellowed.

"It's you who don't know anything. And I'll do what I want."

That was her famous "liberty," but I felt it smashing against me like a log pole in my gut. "God, what a woman you are! You could at least have been considerate enough to tell me about your plans before you took off. I was worried, I had no idea where you were."

"Hah! Hah!" she replied excitedly. "You think just because we lived together for some days and nights that you owe you something. Well, let me tell you: you stayed with me out of fear of breaking your habits, your precious way of life. You want it all but you won't commit to anything. You just want to serve me up for your pleasure whenever you feel like it!"

I shook my head dully and pounded it against the wall. It was painful for me to grasp the meaning of what she was saying.

Feeling somewhat guilty, she tried to explain, "Look, I'm here in some old-British style hotel in Athens. Yes, I'm with Fausto. I want to be here now. I can't answer you, I can't give any guarantees for myself any more. Honestly, I don't know where I'm going, what I'm doing."

"But what about 'us'?"

"Why does it always have to be 'we'? Today it's I and me."

"But do you have to stay with Fausto?"

"He's brilliant, you know. His images are fantastic."

"But will you come back?"

"No promises. I don't want to be made to feel like a prisoner again. Just do what you feel like, what your immediate, true impulses dictate to you, and nothing more. If you want to go out the door, go out the door. Freedom is being able to go out the door whenever you feel like it, without having to answer any questions, explanations, or justifications."

I wanted to tell her that I myself had "gone out the door" many times, but there were many ways of leaving, of coming and going, and finally there was a style that gave a certain dignity to life without which everything became quickly valueless.

Instead, in a voice trembling with rage, I yelled, "You just fled to Athens with Fausto to make love! I really don't give a damn whether you go out the door to go down the street and buy a Tampax or go to the cinema or whatever. For you, all 'going out the door' means is running away to jump into bed with someone else, and that's terrible, it's just not right!"

"Yes, that's exactly right! Last night I screwed Fausto in his ear, can you imagine that?"

"And tomorrow I bet you'll fuck him in his nose."

"Haha! Yes, you're exactly right."

A sudden swell of laughter buoyed her up, then just as abruptly, a wave of sadness overtook her, and she said, "Look, I don't want to hurt you. I don't want us to be saying terrible things to each other, things we will regret, things we really don't mean."

"Right," I affirmed. "I want so much to forgive you, Cynthia. Please come back to me in Paris."

"Darling, O, my poor darling, when are you going to open your eyes and see? You are so good at many things but you don't really understand anything about life, do you? Do you?"

I was silent, not knowing how to respond.

"Be calm, *calmez-vous*," Cynthia hushed me. "Everything is all right. *Tout va bien*. Nothing final has happened yet."

"But will you come back to me?"

"Yes ... no ... or I will try, yes, I will, because I so much want to live—oh, but how?"

CHAPTER 45

▼

I met Ode at a bookstore on the boulevard Montparnasse and we walked to the Luxembourg gardens. Ode had lost weight, had shaved her head again. She looked hard and austere. She said that a few days before she had had to send Jemal back to his father in Casablanca.

"I can understand why Cynthia left," she told me. "She wanted to find another way of being. Life with you was always on a high-tension level. There was too much sexual drama. You let your desire get in the way of pure feeling."

"But what do you think she's doing with Fausto?"

"Don't worry about that. Fausto's only into his own thing. He's completely fascinated by the images he creates, he's really not interested in Cynthia at all, I can assure you."

We walked past the statue of Marechal Ney and reached the latched gates of the "little" Luxembourg gardens.

"You have no family, do you?" asked Ode.

"I haven't seen them in a long time," I said.

She seized my arm, almost hugged me. Glints of April sunshine streaked the well-worn benches.

"Listen to me carefully. You can't hold on to her. You of all people should know there's nothing to hold on to. That's really the supreme art: knowing when to let go."

A young French couple, both in jeans, stood next to the horse chestnut trees in bloom, a few yards away from us, passionately embracing. The shrill cries of school children could be heard farther down the long sandy paths.

"I miss her so much," I murmured. "I want to go to Athens to find her."

"That would be exactly the wrong thing to do. Think of space, the desert, where time is nothing, *rien*, *nada*, it doesn't count."

"I should have been gentle with her. She needed some gentleness. Perhaps I overpowered her."

Now you're just on a guilt trip. That's stupid, *quelle bêtise!*

"The one woman I truly loved, I scared her away," I mused philosophically. "I made her flee. I guess I'm just a bad character."

"Look, a bad character's better than no character at all," Ode tried to cheer me up.

"I can't get her out of my head. She's become like this spirit or phantom who haunts me."

"I have an idea," Ode offered. "You should go see my friend. She's a *voyante*, a seer, she'll tell you about your past, and what's destined in your future."

CHAPTER 46

▼

Mme. Lespinasse, famous *voyante* to André Breton and the surrealist group, in her fifth-floor, walk-up apartment on rue Montmartre, had listened quietly to me for forty-five minutes and now was ready to give me her opinion about Cynthia.

"Astrologically, your girl friend is an Aquarius with an ascendant of Scorpio. Unfortunately, I find that she was also born under the influence of the planet Mars."

"Why unfortunately?"

"Because the Planet Mars, in conjunction with Scorpio rising, contributes to her—how shall I say?—innate destructiveness, a certain nomadic restlessness, while at the same time pushing her in the direction of romantic flirtations."

I thought of Pierre, the fashion photographer, and Ted, the beat poet, and, of course, Charlie, and now Fausto in Athens.

"And how serious are these little affairs?" I wondered.

"Not so much," Mme. Lespinasse continued, now shuffling a deck of Tarot cards. "See, just out of curiosity I pulled some cards for her, and I can tell you that her instinctive impulsiveness, her constant desire for something else, to be *ailleurs*, or elsewhere, make it quite difficult for her to find a stable relationship with any man."

I felt like telling Mme. Lespinasse about Cynthia's "law of three nights," but thought better of it.

"It's doubtful she'll ever marry," Mme. Lespinasse continued. "She won't want to herself, and she'll have no interest in having her own children. In a way, you can see that she's her own creation, and she re-creates herself every day."

I remembered that painful moment with Cynthia when she came back from the American Hospital and told me she was not pregnant. "The world is already full enough, no?" she had tried to rationalize. "And these times don't look particularly bright or promising for the future either, to say the least."

"But," finished Mme. Lespinasse, "you must not forget one very important thing: Cynthia is also under the sign of the planet Uranus, which controls the future. She's following a new path. It isn't easy, and it might not work, but she has no choice but to do it."

She showed me to the door. Her apartment was filled with African masks, plumed feathers, and strange totemic objects. As I left, she flipped a Tarot card and, smiling at me enigmatically, she said, "What do you want? The unexpected always happens. And remember: we're now entering the last cycle, which will be a period of wars, cataclysms, and doom!"

CHAPTER 47

▼

Grateful to be on my own again, I deposited a few hundred franc notes in her outstretched palm. But I knew that my days in Paris were numbered. Without Cynthia, I had nowhere to go, no real *raison d'être*. What I had learned in Paris was how to connect with another being. But now there were only fragments of a remembered life, such as the afternoon I went walking with her outside Paris in the Bois de Boulogne. She had climbed onto a narrow stone wall; there was a forty-foot drop below. Perched precariously on one leg, she had remarked, "It's all a question of balance. You see? There always has to be some danger." And with her head thrown back as far as it would go, her arms crossed behind her, chin up, her eyes closed, she had begun to walk forward.

For a few days, I stayed mostly in my room, thinking about Cynthia and her friends, about what I had loved and lost. Then the concierge slipped a rare letter under the door that was postmarked Cairo, Egypt. It was handwritten in large, clear letters on sand-colored papyrus paper.

> *My Dearest You,*
>
> *Don't ask me again to say anything or to explain why I left. You've known for some time that I can't read books any more or think logically. I don't know what's the matter with me. I just need to feel and live. When I was in Istanbul I found some poems by this Turkish poet, Rumi. He was a whirling dervish, a wise man. Poems are perhaps the most important thing of all—they "mean," they've got soul ...*
>
> *I feel so many people want something from me. I'm just tired of it all, tired of having things thrown at me. We've heard it all before. Man has proved, achieved himself. How much farther can he go?*

Perhaps I'm just sick of language and talk. I want to live very quietly, simply, and truly. That's all.

Anyway, it's four forty-five in the morning here. I'm staying in a beautiful old English-style hotel near the Nile. I'm having a hard time. It seems I've been awake eternally, born, died and come back to some place again. I imagine you in Paris on rue Campagne-lrè, are you still there? Am I free? What am I doing here in Cairo? Am I going completely nuts? Who's that man sleeping there on the bed? Fausto? Even he puts pressure on me.

Hmmm, let's see what the bargain is. I'm a woman. In a country like this I'm supposed to stay in the house and keep the fire burning, the food warm. In Paris I was supposed to go out with men, look pretty, smile and say yes ...

Why do people treat each other this way? Do they really think they're helping? Am I expecting roses? If freedom is knowing what you want, then I think Charlie is free. You're not free yet, because you haven't found out exactly what you want. I seem to be free, but actually I'm not, because I'm not doing anything except traveling around the world and letting Fausto shoot me every day with his camera and never let me see what he's doing.

Ah, what a mess my head is—what a bordello, *no? And some people publish shit like this.*

Art is only for a moment—just to clear one's head and to help, hopefully, to live a little better. Or am I missing the point? Sometimes I think I'm missing the whole G.D. point of everything.

Many of the things we do to each other seem done in love but are actually done out of fear. Perhaps I'm being too rough, but I'm trying to see things clearly because I'm not feeling as well as I'd like. I think out of a fear of losing me, you were always interrupting me, demanding too much of me. But I mean, love should automatically include honoring the other person's needs, wants. I think most men are guilty of this—from the beginning of time woman is supposed to serve man— extol, support, give to him. Each complements the other, okay, but I'm sure women have not been given due respect as human beings. I'm not a feminist. I think I'm being fair.

I don't want to give up anything any more to anyone. I don't want to be in a situation where we're each hurting each other and limiting our freedom rather than extending it. Right now I'm a little tired of traveling, fatigué. *I'm also upset that I should always be made to feel guilty for living spontaneously at the tips of my fingers.*

One must be able to go in and out of the door when one wants. There are no guarantees or securities. That's why marriage has never rung true to me even though I've desired it from time to time desperately. And I was so heartbroken that day I went to the American Hospital and thought I was pregnant with your child, but I wasn't ...

We are in a new age—I'm sure of it. I'm part of It, but it's very difficult, and very often I wish I weren't. I don't know how to live. I'm having one hell of a time and I'm not cracking my skull over the question at every second. But it's there.

Please be my friend and don't try to force me one way or another. I guess I don't understand much about anything, but I do need my friends. Be patient with this traveling turtle. I'm off to bed, to try to sleep. Fausto just asked again what I'm doing. Hmmm?

CHAPTER 48

▼

Jean-François called. He told me over lunch that he had found some new Middle Eastern investors for his "dynamic living center."

I remembered what Cynthia had said about Jean-François, "Here's a man who's trying to find freedom for everyone but doesn't know enough to be able to give it to himself."

I remembered many other things about her, how she liked to get up early in the morning to go to the Marché Saint-Pierre to buy fabric. Making her own clothes had always been one of her own things, a style she lived by, a manner of the grace she gave. Closing my eyes, I could easily see her prancing semi-nude on the balcony of our loft, being careful not to step on all the new fabric and tissues. One night she had cooked me a simple dinner of whole brown rice and artichoke hearts, flavored with salt and pepper and sunflower oil and vinegar. We both had started sucking at the leaves.

"How do you cook artichokes?" she had looked up and asked me.

"In boiling water, of course."

"Like green lobsters," she said.

Often, after making love, she could not fall asleep. She'd go downstairs, put on some music. Sometimes she would play the flute or start singing to herself. Then she would urge me to get up, to join her, to be with her in some way, in that nighttime period between one and three in the morning of indefinite, lazy madness.

One such night I muttered, "If the concierge next door hears you, she's going to raise hell tomorrow morning."

Cynthia came back to bed, the sheets now pulled up to her bare shoulders. "I just don't care! That concierge, that old bag! That old big hag bag! Let her go and live with the cows in the country if she doesn't want to hear noises."

Now, alone again, not knowing where I was, in what strange city or even what geography, I realized I had come to Paris to find something I had not lived before. I had found it, I had possessed it for a moment, but now again it had eluded me, and I was left with the memory of what had been.

If that memory pursued me like a phantom, it also bothered Charlie and kept him from doing his work. Over drinks at Le Coupole, he told me how hard it was for him to focus on his new series of paintings, which later became famous as the *Women on Horseback*.

"Look, pal," Charlie told me in a strong, clear voice, "there's no point in being sentimental. That's the worst mistake you can make. Things are what they are. Life's made up of a very few basic needs. That's all. *C'est tout.* Life's so simple, so very simple."

If it was as simple as that, I wondered, why was I having such a hard time of it? Why couldn't I just forget about her and go on to something else? Instead, my head continued to fill with flashbacks of her; for example, the day she had come out in a clown costume stomping up and down, looking as stupid and goofy as possible. She had encouraged me to light a candle and run after her, trying to set fire to her elusive *derrière*. And once, at a midnight surprise party, she had pretended to consume large quantities of Dom Perignon champagne, "Glug, glug, glug," before falling down in a liquid, contorted heap and hugging my legs desperately, as if to say, "You must get me out of here. You are responsible for my well-being."

At other times she would stay hunched for hours over her gun-gray sewing machine, absorbed in the task of working with material and transforming fabric into exquisite flowing patterns, "bright, pleasant houses for the body to live in," as she used to say.

Spontaneously, gaily, she called out, "Come, pretend you're a cat. Put your head on my neck and your paws on—"

Those were the good moments when she was in a mood of joyous tenderness and receptivity. Her flesh shone softly, her body was open, clear and sweet, and I caressed it dreamily until she cried out, "Be a tiger cat, jump me!"

I seized her. I felt I could establish some electrical connection with her inner soul.

"Your nose is going to drown in me," she protested.

But I continued, plunging ahead, smelling the blonde fragile fragrance of her flesh I knew so well.

"Miaowww," she purred. "Miaowww. Hahaha!" She laughed in expansive, happy bursts.

"Do it again!" she demanded, like a child.

Later, sprawled on the Moroccan cushions after a peasant dinner of fresh black olives, goat cheese, a *baguette*, and red wine, I watched as she danced for me, the lights dimmed, her arched body towering above me, her fine hair ablaze like straw, her every motion vibrant and incandescent.

"Cock on the wall! Cock cock a whoodle whoo!" she cried gleefully, springing up, as if immune to gravity.

"Get up," she urged. "Don't just lie there and watch me. Bounce like a toy, be rubber." She wavered around me in bright, leafy circles.

"Forget your past loves. You don't need them."

"But why forget all the things that made me who I am?"

"Why do you try to preserve yourself? Just let yourself go, let yourself be peeled."

For a moment, then, we had known true freedom; it was wild, infinitely playful, and outside of time.

I remembered how, teasing her, I had called her "the eternal ephemeral." But now she was gone, she was traveling with Fausto—she was in Athens, Istanbul, Cairo, or Kyoto.

Perhaps I could have done something that would have prevented her from leaving. Perhaps it was true that I had been too possessive. Perhaps it was true that I hadn't been gentle enough with her, or that I had sought to exert too much control over her mind and body. But it didn't matter. Nothing mattered. For others, Paris would always be Paris, but for me Paris would never stop being what I had lived with Cynthia.

CHAPTER 49

▼

"Another drink?" Charlie asked. We were sitting on the barstools at the Rosebud on rue Delambre. It was well after midnight. I declined. Charlie poured himself another shot.

"I just don't get it," he said. "Cynthia said she loved you. She told that to me, to me! It was all so simple. And now, now this—she just split without a word."

"We were becoming too close—something like family. To her it was a threat."

"Yeah, kiddo, maybe she was right, we're always trying to establish relationships that make us prisoners. We do the most desperate and crazy things just in order to be able to feel attached. Then we fool ourselves by calling it love. Love's brief, it's an intensity, it can't last. Sooner or later life takes over, comes crashing down with all its heavy demands."

Charlie lit a Lucky Strike. "Incredible," he went on. "*La vie est bizarre*. But there's never any telling in advance—predictions aren't allowed. It's like painting. When I make the first stroke, I'm free to do that, but I never know what's going to happen, to come out afterwards. But you should understand her, you've got an adventurous spirit. She felt a need to sniff the air, that little girl, to cleanse, to purify herself in space, to soar, to find a new freedom."

I nodded. I wondered if she would ever find the clarity she was looking for. Charlie asked the barman for another Black Label and soda.

"She's with that Italian film-maker Fausto who's supposed to be making a movie about her, something about developing a new relationship with time and space."

"Space and time," Charlie said. "You know, pal, I got a letter today from Cynthia. Want to read it?"

"A letter from Cynthia?" I was amazed. "Where was it from?"

"I think it was from California. Here, read it," and Charlie handed me a neatly folded white page filled with her clear, rounded handwriting.

> *Dear Charlie,*
>
> *I had to leave Paris. Please know I'm not angry with you or with anyone. I'm simply exhausted and empty. I simply cannot accept the way in which people plunge to the depths of one another until they are bare, exposed and utterly open. In the Western way I cannot accept it, nor perhaps in any way. I refuse to be possessed, enraged with your anguish, and perhaps loved ...*
>
> *You're an artist. With you I would perhaps know myself eventually. But you never left me to myself, nor left anything untouched, and it was beautiful but terrible, and I feel so drained.*
>
> *I can't see anyone for a while until I've gained my equilibrium and peace. I'm going to Arizona tomorrow and I just want to be alone there and mistress of myself ...*

The letter ended abruptly. It was not even signed, as if somehow she had not even had the strength to attach her name to her thoughts.

She's not free yet," said Charlie. "That last bit of freedom, the most difficult, she still has to win. Maybe she'll do it there in that big American desert near the Grand Canyon."

I looked at Charlie's face. There was an intensity to his features approaching desperation, a ravaging.

"In the end, if you want her, you're going to have to go get her. You're going to have to take the good with the bad, man. It's all one package."

"Ha! I wish I could," I said.

"Another drink?" He filled his glass with whisky. "You can do it, kid. Go live the rest of your life. And no looking back over your shoulder—no rearview mirror acts."

It was raining hard outside—rain lashing the dull Paris pavements.

"Take care of yourself, Charlie." I rose to leave.

"Me? I'm just an old man. Old man, me, *moi*. I'm not hoping for anything any more. If something comes, it's wonderful, but I have no illusions. I'm not expecting or waiting for anything or anyone."

In the shadow of a shuttered café, a *clochard* was urinating over the curb. The rain fell. It was windy, and clouds whipped over the chimney-pot rooftops hiding the moon.

The bum suddenly swerved and grabbed me with his arms, as if to embrace me, but almost knocked me down.

"Hey, what the hell! Leave me alone, you bastard."

The drunk graciously bowed and moved out of the way, tipping his crushed hat.

I walked down the long, tree-shrouded boulevard. It was my last night in Paris. Tomorrow I would fly to Arizona in search of Cynthia. Now I just wanted to focus my mind and energies on the woman who, in this special city, had been so much a part of our lives. Back in the studio, I filled a brandy glass, set it down on the solitary table, lit a candle, and sat for a long time in the darkness. Cynthia appeared around me in whorls of multiple phantoms. Her much-loved face was everywhere. In a few minutes I felt she would scratch at the window like a cat, and I would open it, and she would be there.

CHAPTER 50

▼

When the phone rang early the next morning, it was Judy.

"Did you hear the terrible news?"

"No, what?"

"Cynthia's dead."

"Dead? No, no, it can't be."

"There was an automobile accident near Sedona. Apparently she was driving up there on the cliffs along a narrow road, and the road curved, but she kept going straight. They found the car in a ravine."

"I don't believe it."

"She was alone in the car. They don't know what happened—whether she lost control, or … But she just kept going straight, and the road curved, and then—"

"What about Fausto?"

"He was waiting for her in some hotel in Sedona. They were supposed to go do some filming at sunset out on the red cliffs. Cynthia had gone to check it out."

"And what happens now?"

"I don't know. Her body's being sent back to family members in New Hampshire." Judy paused. I could hear her crying softly. "You should never have let her go. You should have stopped her at all costs—hit her, been violent with her. Yes, you should have woken her up with a good slap, got her out of the fantasy world she was in, broken the cycle."

"That's completely absurd. I could never act like that, and anyway, she would have split in a second."

"Often I want to leave," Judy said, "but Jean-François just grabs me, hits me, and afterwards I'm somehow glad."

"I don't want to talk about it right now," I said.

"By the way, did you know that I'm pregnant?"

"Pregnant?"

"Yes, it's a boy. Jean-François wants to call him Vladimir, after Lenin. You know how political he is."

A few days later the concierge slipped a postcard from Sedona, Arizona, under the door. Postmarked a few days earlier, and written in her clear, well-formed handwriting, it said simply:

I want nothing but what goes forward. Bless you, bless you.

I also received this letter from Ode:

> *I heard about Cynthia's tragic death in Arizona. Frankly, it cannot be called tragic because she was a woman who wanted to explore all the boundaries of life. Many people did not understand her, but she always followed her own path. I'll never forget those early days when she was doing those magazine photos and we traveled around in North Africa. No, she was my good friend, a true companion to my own soul, and I will never forget her.*
>
> *As for me, guess what? I'm in love, can you believe it? I met this marvelous oriental man. He's an emir—a Turkish prince—and he took me to Istanbul. I made him promise to give me a separate house so we won't actually live together, and in this way avoid the compromises that always kill love. Say a prayer for my happiness, as I will say a silent prayer for the love I know you had for Cynthia.*

It was hard for me to rationalize the feelings of loss that Cynthia's death had stirred up. In spite of my pain, I found in some way I envied Cynthia because she had had the courage to act, to free herself of her desires by fulfilling them—acting out everything and finally liberating herself even from love. For a radiant moment in Paris, she and I had coincided. In that sense, there was really no such thing as loss. From now on I knew I would simply have to be strong enough to create joy out of absence, as, with her death, it had become clear how easily convertible absence and presence are, how swiftly and subtly they merge the one into the other.

CHAPTER 51

▼

I had heard that Fausto Arditi was back in Paris, and a few weeks later, by chance at an opening at the Galerie Sonnabend for the American painter Robert Rauschenberg, I ran into him. I was anxious to see the film he had made about their *Voyage from East to West*. Those would be the last images of her life. I wondered if he had taken any shots of her in Sedona.

Fausto seemed almost relieved to see me. He said he had made an incredible film about Cynthia, and, if I wanted to see it, that would be his pleasure, it could be easily arranged. I sensed that Fausto was suffering as well from Cynthia's loss, and he was eager to share the film he had done with someone else whom he knew had cared deeply about her.

"You know, by the time we got to Arizona, there wasn't much left of the money Dominique de Montagu had given us—maybe only a few thousand dollars. We didn't need it any more, so the day before Cynthia died, we left it in a trash bin in a Mobil gas station. Cynthia wanted to be free of it. But can you imagine the look on the face of the guy who found it?"

Fausto had feared that Cynthia's family, or even the Montagu clan, would try to take possession of the film, so he had stored it for safety in a "troglodytic apartment" he had rented. I found out that this wasn't so much an apartment as a furnished cave, built into the chalk cliffs that rose over the Loire River. It was in a remote area, beautiful but very isolated, and I was to meet him there that weekend. Saturday morning I rented a car—a blue Peugeot—and drove to Rochecorbon in the Loire valley.

The "troglodyte house" was accessibly by stone steps that wound up the steep side of a cliff. I had to leave the car at a bus stop parking lot off the main road a mile or so away. It was late afternoon when I arrived, and I was surprised and concerned to find there was no electricity or running water. This "apartment" had literally been carved into the chalk walls of the massive cliff, no doubt hundreds of years ago.

"How are we going to watch the film?" I asked Fausto.

"Not to worry," he said, perfectly at ease. "When night falls, we'll use candles and gas lanterns. Cynthia would have liked it that way, don't you think?"

The blue ribbon of the Loire river was reflected through the overhanging embankment foliage. We could see it far below as we trekked through the neighboring fields to buy some food for dinner from the local farmers. We came back with some fresh tomatoes, goat cheese, bread, and wine. It was simple and primitive. I really didn't care because my only purpose in coming was to see the film about Cynthia—her last trip.

The tomatoes were ripe and full and tasted good as we huddled in the cave and ate the bread and fresh cheese. The sun went down, it grew quickly cool, and you could feel the dampness seeping out of the ancient stone walls. I kept waiting for Fausto to show me the film, but he seemed in no hurry. "It doesn't last long," he told me. "Only a few minutes."

A powerful surge of adrenalin rose in me, because Cynthia had been traveling for almost two weeks. It didn't seem logical that any series of images about her could be compressed into such a short time span.

Fausto finally managed to arrange some electrical connection with a neighboring cave.

"Are you ready?" he asked.

It was very dark now. The only light in the cave came from the guttering candles and a few gas lanterns. A reel of film in the movie projector was going to display the images on the uneven walls of the cave.

I nodded. I felt tense and hard and coiled. It was not easy to control my growing anger.

"When you watch these images," Fausto said, "don't think about what happened before them, what led up to them, or even what they mean. Don't let the past or the future influence what you're going to watch now. Never do that, never! As I always told Cynthia, just pay attention to what's in front of your nose."

I was about ready to punch him. Dark rage and regret filled my mind. It was hard to believe that I was alone with this gaunt, bearded Italian film-maker in an old stone cave chiseled by time's effects out of a centuries-old cliff face.

"I loved Cynthia," Fausto was saying. "I know that you loved her too. If she hadn't died, she would have come back to you, you know, because it really was too late for her to leave. I think she left to try to prove to herself that it wasn't … I told her that, but she wouldn't listen to me. She was young, enthusiastic—yes, even innocent. She thought she could do anything. Oh, what a woman she was! What a character! But now, you see, it's really too late, it's just too late."

"What are you getting at, damn it! Just show me the goddamned film!"

The film began to whirr through a Kodak projector, and on the rough-hewn white shadowy walls of the cave, lit eerily by the gas lamps and rows of candles, images started to flicker. I looked for the images of Cynthia I knew so well—her clear blue shining eyes, her smooth oval face, her laughing blonde hair, her svelte, dancing, elusive body.

But on the scratched ragged walls of the cave, all that was visible, all that could be seen, was the outline of Cynthia's bare hand moving back and forth, up and down, in slow and ever-widening circles, in front of the camera lens, creating a series of rapidly changing black-and-white semi-abstract images.

"You wasted her, you killed her, you bastard!" I shouted, my voice reverberating off the thick cave walls.

"No, man, you've got it wrong—this is reality, the real thing, and you know what it is? It's a flicker, a brief moment between light and darkness, a vibration of black and white that you can fast-forward or watch in slow motion, as you like. In terms of the millions of years of human existence, we're not even an image, we're no more than the outline of a shadow, like Cynthia's hand moving in front of my camera lens, a dizzying succession of absence/presence, light/darkness, fullness/void, here/hereafter, life/death …"

What happened next, happened quickly, and never has been totally clear to me. I know there was a fierce struggle and candles toppling over, and the gas lamps shattering, furniture being thrown, and then the cave quickly filling up with smoke, the cave on fire. I managed to run out and lurch down the narrow stone steps to the bottom of the cliff. Stumbling and bruised, I found my way to the car I had left in the bus stop parking lot.

CHAPTER 52

▼

It took me some time to recover. I got a job at a major art gallery translating all their catalogs into English. I was able to rent the same duplex studio at 23, rue Campagne-Irè that I'd had before. It was hard for me to believe all that had happened. For me, the trouble with her death was that she hadn't truly died. Her image stayed with me and kept popping up out of corners and winking at me at odd moments. I could see her freed of anxiety, rooted in a new strength, wild and frail, raw and blonde, laughing unpredictably, saying, "But it's not possession that counts."

"She had a violence," I told her old friend, Gloria, who was visiting from London. "Perhaps not the most violence, but I can see her carrying the shock, the wave, of our generation. She lived out the whole thing. There are some people who seem to have just one wave in them—one violence. They have this one incredible thing to live and then they go away …"

"Yes," said Gloria. "It wasn't even that Cynthia had something important to say. The important things in her were her gestures, her attitude, the way she behaved, moved, the aura she created around her. It was like electricity, a kind of magical vibration that you felt at once."

"I just never thought she'd have the courage to leave as she did," I said.

"I didn't either. But you can't play. You can't say, 'I'll try it for a little while and see.' She did it absolutely, all the way to the end. The little girl, she escaped us forever!"

I remembered the day she and I had gone out for a walk around Saint-Germain-des-Prés, revisiting the places we had known. We had walked around the church of Saint-Germain-des-Prés, then turned down rue de l'Abbaye. "I've lived a little more than twenty years," she had said, "and nothing was good until I came to Paris and met you. It was so wonderful that we were together and that we were young in Paris, that we had that—something that no one can ever take away from us no matter what happens to either of us." Her voice broke. She'd begun to cry a little bit.

"Don't, don't," I had urged her softly. "Come on, please."

"There's something in me that's always wishing for more." She stopped. She looked at me with her clear gray-blue eyes. "And there's something in me that's always wishing for you."

I held her. I hugged her. I remember that as the sweetest and most anguished embrace I ever had.

I had come to Paris as a "country boy from Buffalo." I had learned many things from Cynthia. I had learned how to love and I had learned that love can survive in loss and can even grow and thrive in loss, and that ultimately there is no loss.

I saw Charlie one more time. The news of her death had hit him hard. "Maybe she found that fourth dimension she was always looking for," he smiled grimly.

"Perhaps. I think that more and more she knew she was living in a new world, radically different from anything that preceded it. And she was knocking herself over the head trying to find a way of living within it."

"I'm just an old man," Charlie said. "I don't understand. I don't get it. Perhaps I don't want to get it any more. I thought I could find a freedom beyond my work. But now I realize that work is the most important thing of all. There's nothing else. A man is what he does."

"A man becomes what he is," I answered.

Charlie smiled. "Look, kiddo, I told you in the beginning, I'm a deluxe bum, an elegant drunk. I know I mumble a bit, I don't think too clearly. It was stupid of me to have gotten so involved with her, but she was like a worm in my head. Oh, she was a great girl. And no, what happened to her, I just don't get it. I'm sorry, kiddo, if I upset you or anything. I told you before, if you want to shoot me, I'll buy you the gun."

"No, Charlie, you don't have to do that."

"It's finished for me anyway here. I'm going back to Connecticut. I've got a barn there and deer that come across the land early in the morning, and I'm going to take care of my daughter and paint and drink a little and that's all … good-bye."

"Good-bye, Charlie."

Our eyes met. I looked into his dark, rugged, gangster face. There was tenderness there; there was a love.

At the door Charlie suddenly did something I had never seen him do before: he started crying. The tears flowed. His big, strong body jerked. He was helpless, a child. "Not her!" he yelled. "Not Cynthia!" Then he groaned, he sighed violently, bitterly, and he howled.

After that, life changed rapidly. I knew it was time to move on. Paris was exhausted for me. There was nothing left "to live." All that I had lived I could take with me in my head. Cynthia would have been proud of me: the only possession I needed from now on was my warehouse of memories.

Meanwhile, Ode had returned from Istanbul, where her relationship with the Turkish prince had not lasted.

I met her for coffee one afternoon at Le Coupole. We sat on the leather benches surrounded by the tall columns decorated with the murals done by Picasso and Modigliani. I ordered a *petit-crème* and Ode said, "You look dazed. Don't fight it. Be grateful for what you had. It's so short, and, the way we live, it's even shorter. It's going to end soon, time is running out, we've poisoned the earth, sickened our minds. We kill ourselves with how we live, with everything we do. We're our own assassins, and it's not even amusing, that's the terrible thing … So think of what you had with Cynthia. Even a few months of happiness can be so important, enormous! Just one great love and everything is saved. The poles are going to shift as we enter the fourth cycle. Perhaps it's not so bad that it ended the way it did."

I said goodbye to Ode. I never saw her again. A few weeks went by.

It was a warm misty night in early April. I thought I heard footsteps on the cobbled passageway. Then there was a sound as if someone were scratching at the widow. The scratching continued, soft and insistent. I opened the window.

Cynthia was outside. She said nothing. She just stood and looked at me, like a phantom.

"Cynthia, Cynthia!" I cried. "Why don't you come in?"

She shook her head slowly. Her pale, smooth, oval face assumed a look of radiant, wistful beauty. She looked at me and kept shaking her head softly, whispering the words, "No, no, it's better this way, it's better, you'll see. One day you'll understand, you will, I promise you, but don't try to bring me back from the other side, don't try to remember me, what was, was. Just let it be, please, for me."

The next morning was gray and foggy. I took a taxi to Orly Airport and flew back to New York City.

978-0-595-48658-8
0-595-48658-4

Printed in the United States
115359LV00004B/309/P

9 780595 486588